Christine Sanni

Meet Me
At The
Table

Where Greatness & Impact Collide

MEET ME AT THE TABLE
WHERE GREATNESS AND IMPACT COLLIDE

An empowering guide to create positive impact at every table. A strong call to identifying the value you bring to your work and the critical choice you must make in an era where product is no longer your highest currency.

CHRISTINE SANNI
YOUR GREATNESS COACH

Printed in the United States of America
Environmental Notice: Printed on SFI Certified paper.
First Edition

Website: www.christinesanni.com

ISBN 978-1-09830-602-1 eBook 978-1-09830-603-8

To my best friend, my confidant, the first person that made me believe in my own greatness, my soulmate, my husband, ikhelowa Sanni, Thank you. I could not have accomplished this without you. You were there with me, through every chapter, through every late night and early morning. I will never forget the sacrifice you have made to make this a reality.

I love you.

To our family. To running towards all of our dreams. To our journey. And to beginning again.

Contents

RIGHT NOW, AT THIS MOMENT...

I sit with you. There was no way to have predicted our meeting, but here we are, side by side. Like you, I have been in pursuit of my life's meaning and purpose. I've had moments of settling; of giving up; and of extreme effort; but even then, I was unable to piece it all together. This book details the moment my life changed, how I came to understand the greatest parts of me, and how I applied them to my life. It will serve as a guide to help you too, understand the greatest parts of who you are.

Those unique qualities, gifts, and passions that you may be keeping secret, but literally burn a hole into the vision you have for yourself, each and every day. It is these pieces that perhaps others highlight in conversation and spark something deep within you. But even then, they are too scary to acknowledge or pursue. Instead, it becomes easier to change the subject, most times with lingering disappointment that someone else has so easily acknowledged a gift you do have, but have yet to release to the world. I get it…

I've been there…

I have lived much of my life feeling incapable of creating what I could not often put into words, let alone into action. It wasn't until I decided. I made a choice, and that choice changed the rest of my life. The outcome of my future and my happiness came down to one decision. I made the choice that the scariest thing on earth to me was not that I would fail at something I truly loved and desired to explore, but that those who were meant to be touched by my journey, my pain, my message, and my work, wouldn't have that opportunity, because I was simply too afraid to fail at who I was destined to become.

I couldn't let that happen. Here we are. Born into a world with unlimited possibilities, unlimited opportunities to get it wrong, but also get it right. I came to understand that the greatest part of being human was not what my success could buy, but just how much impact I could create if I was willing to simply **give**. To make the world a better place because I could. No matter your start, journey, career, race, religion, sexual orientation, or self-identification, what matters most is that you make the most of who you are right now, in this lifetime. That you discover all of who you are; take your rightful seat at the table; and understand that your existence even to this point, has been nothing short of a miracle.

There are no mistakes when it comes to your existence. This means, you have something to **give** and even though you may at times not feel it, that does not negate the fact you were born with a purpose. This is a very special moment for you and me. Because the greatest part of our connection, here and now, is that our paths have brought us together; unplanned but timely; unexpected, but destined.

I wrote this book so that I would be here, waiting for you as you take your seat. To tell you that you are not alone in your pursuit... to tell you that even if you doubt yourself, there is nothing you cannot accomplish. That, whatever you have been through before this moment, will never be bigger than what you will create in the future. I'm so thankful for this moment. As you read, may you be inspired to discover the deepest parts of you - to understand those things that create your value, the purpose of your existence, and what you will **give** to the world.

This book, for some, will represent the boardroom you walk into but have yet to let your voice be heard; the familiar conversations where you have yet to express who you truly are; a life where you have yet to **give**. When you are done reading *Meet Me At The Table*, and you have made the decision to never look back, all I ask is that you share this book with as many people as you can and be there waiting for them, as they too take their seats. Are you ready? If so, I invite you to...

CHAPTER 1

TAKE YOUR SEAT

I remember the feeling that rushed through me…a feeling of clarity as to how I would live the rest of my life. Not just a choice but also a commitment to **give** instead of take. For the first time, I felt unstoppable; empowered to face the world head-on. My perspective had surely changed. I knew that the world wasn't going to just happen to me, but I was going to happen to the world. I was pushed naturally, quite instinctively, to shed the negative thoughts that I had told myself for so long. It became clear to me that none of them were true.

As a child in school, I remember hearing the teachers tell us "sticks and stones may break our bones but words will never break you." That couldn't be further from the truth. Words are powerful. Especially the ones we **give** ourselves. The labels I had placed on myself for so many years, did hurt me. They were preventing me from living, exploring, and creating. From **giving** my best at home and at work. I lived every day as a victim of every single word that played in my mind. I had to change and it all started with my mindset. I had to know and believe that I belonged at the table.

You've got to know you belong...

In order for you to take your seat, the only way you are coming to the room is by knowing and believing you belong in the room. This first chapter will dive into the mindset and what it takes to embrace your failures.

What is Mindset?

Simply put, your mindset is what you tell yourself you are. That means anything you say you are, whether aloud or subconsciously, you believe. You may ask, Christine "Well, what about what others say that I am?" I would say the only weight those words hold, are the ones that you actually believe.

What do you believe? Who do you believe you are? Because, that is the only thing that matters when it comes to creating the rest of your life, knowing exactly who you are. There is no other place to start... no other place to start from than with your mindset.

Your mindset will either bring you to the table or prevent you from walking into the room. You either believe you can't or believe you can. Many refer to the mindset as '**Fixed vs. Growth**.' I call it **Boxed vs. Open**. Each and every day, I choose not to live my life boxed into what society thinks I'm capable of, but rather, what only I can imagine I'm capable of. I'm **Open** to the unknown; what I have yet to envision, explore, and create. And so...

Your mindset becomes your greatest asset.

Boxed vs. Open

Let's look at these two mindsets closely and how you can transition from one to the other.

Boxed Mindset

If you're connected with me on LinkedIn you've seen this quote: *Limitation comes when you have accepted that there is nothing beyond what is visible. Success happens when you create what is beyond.* Having a boxed mindset assumes that your growth and evolution at some point, become static; and that there is nothing else beyond what you have already achieved.

I liken this to the times I chose to accept that I could not give more to my work, outside of my job description, or when I used to tell myself, "I'm just a mother, I'm just a wife there is no way I can pursue my passions. Not now, not ever." **Remember**, *labels are powerful*. Every time I told myself I could not, I did not; and continued to live within the boxes that I created. Have you ever felt like you were trapped, boxed in, with no way out? I have. And making the choice to **give** to humanity for the rest of my life, was me climbing out of every box, I had ever lived in.

Open Mindset

Having an **open** mindset is the exact opposite of living life, boxed in. It is the second half of my quote. *Success **does** happen when you create what is beyond.* Living life completely **open** to what you have yet to envision, explore, and create. It's being comfortable with everything unknown. It is understanding that learning is continuous and the more you know, the more you can create.

I could go on and on because being **open**-minded, is creating without limits and therefore, living a limitless life. It's important that I take this moment to share with you an important realization I came to, in order for me to change my mindset. Being **open**-minded did and does not mean I would not fail or experience hard times throughout my journey. I had, in fact, overcome so many things that once filled me with discouragement, self-doubt, and pain.

Being **open**-minded meant that even if I failed, even if bad things happened to me, they did not define me. Being **open**-minded is the realization that those things make you stronger; they qualify you for the next phase of your life, the exploration of your journey. It's just like taking a test. The answers are not included. The test may knock you down, it may be hard to navigate, and you may even fail it. But when the time comes, and it will, you become better equipped to handle the next one.

If you have not failed; if you have not fallen down, you will not have the tools that are required to take your seat, not just once, but again and again. We'll talk more about this later on in the book, but for now, I want to level-set and clearly set expectations. I'm not telling you that you will never fail or have the fear of failing. You will, but the worst that can happen is that you reach, miss your mark, and grow in the process.

If you have started to be introspective while reading this chapter, and want to know if you have lived your life Boxed in or **Open**, here are some questions you may want to ask yourself:

- *Do you believe you can change?*

- *Do you believe in personal development?*

- *Do you believe in hard work and do you understand its value?*

- *Do you listen to your inner voice?*

If the answer to any of these questions is no or you feel you can relate to what I have shared, then the great news is, you have the opportunity to **open** yourself up to limitless possibilities from this point forward, in all that you do; your family, your work, and your passions.

If you're asking yourself; is it possible to change my mindset at this point in my life? Absolutely.

There is a vast amount of research that has been done and shows we all have the power to change our mindset.

What is neuroplasticity?

Allow me to give you the science behind what we are discussing. Neuroscience refers to Neuroplasticity as cognitive change. Neuroplasticity is the ability of the human brain to experience 'lifelong' change and rewire itself, as a result of learning new material and experiencing new events. In fact, as you read this, your brain is being rewired, changed to **open** yourself up to the idea that it's never too late to learn something new. So, don't ever doubt your ability to form new understanding and therefore a new mindset.

Boxed to Open; the Transition

Earlier, I shared with you that I made a very important decision as to how I would live my life moving forward. That meant, my transition started with the act of deciding. Your life, up until this point, has brought you to many forks in the road. What you would eat; what you would wear; who you would be in a relationship with. Some easier than others, but still, decisions that were made. After I made my decision to **give**, I began to work on my mindset and how I saw my life. I started out with what I perceived as failures.

I embraced my failures

Like you, I too, have a story. One that I'll share more deeply in another book. For now, you should know that I have not been immune to trauma, mistakes, & failure in my lifetime. If you had met me whilst I was in the midst of them, I would tell you I didn't see the "light at the end of the tunnel." I did not know that from each of my trials, my greatest reward wouldnot be that I made it through them, but what I had gained from them. My strength...My fortitude...My empathy... My inspiration...And if you ask me now, "Christine, how do you feel about all that you have experienced?" I would tell you that my scars have made and make me unstoppable.

My trauma, taught me forgiveness; my mistakes taught me, what not to do; and my failures taught me how to do it better the next time. I have fully embraced my journey.

There may be so many people who you admire. The question becomes; do you admire them for their success now or for how they carried on despite their failures? An interesting perspective. I think about someone like Steven Spielberg who experienced rejection from film school; not once, but three times, before his big break. I admire him less for his movies and more for his ability to create some of the world's best blockbusters, despite recurrent rejection.

Open instead of boxed...

I think about Oprah Winfrey. She built one of the world's most recognized talk shows, but did you know that she was fired from the Baltimore TV station WJZ-TV? Her producer reportedly told her "you are unfit for television news." Bring on the labels. Imagine if she had believed the label of being "unfit." I admire her more for her ability to live outside of any label that was thrown her way.

Open instead of boxed...

Ask yourself... How do I see my failures now that I'm on the other side of them?

Trials are not designed to determine our worth, but to demonstrate our transformative strength. Living life **Open**. Below, I share how I embraced my failures:

- *I let go:* I could not change what had already occurred: I let go of the 'could haves,' 'would haves,' and 'should haves' and focused on what I could create moving forward. The only way to make room for what you have to **give** and **create** in the future is to let go of what you cannot change.

Take Your Seat...

- *I redirected my focus:* I focused on what I could **give** to my family and work moving forward. I began to look forward, instead of behind me. I was finally going in a different direction. I began to align with my natural compass. It wasn't always north, but it was forward and forward felt right. It felt timely. It felt deserving. I realized how tired I really was; constantly feeding the need to look behind me. I had a sense of direction and I began to tell myself that my failures only pushed me forward, not backward.

Take Your Seat...

- *I got feedback from those I trusted:* For me, these individuals were my family and my mentors. I will acknowledge that there will be plenty of people with opinions on how you should let go. Trust your gut here. If you feel like someone is giving you constructive feedback to genuinely help you, then listen closely. If you feel that the advice you are getting is misguided and leaves you feeling more negative than you did before, it should go in one ear and out the other.

At this stage, something quite unexpected began to happen. With every opportunity to share my failures and my experiences, I became stronger. Quite unexpected on many fronts. Those I shared my story with, found familiarity, and we created a safe space for each other to be **open** and honest about what we had gone through - An inspiring story of triumph between us, in a place where judgment could not be felt. The more I shared, the more I realized I could move forward and let go.

Take Your Seat...

- ***I gave failure a new definition:*** Failure was no longer finite to me. I redefined failure as being both necessary and temporary. As indicative of so many, I realized my life had been a living example that failure was where I grew the most and that when I experienced failure, it was always temporary. Isn't that true for everyone's life? Do storms truly last forever?

Take Your Seat...

I Acknowledged Inspiration...

- ***My Life Up Until That Point:*** When I lived life boxed in, I saw everything wrong that happened throughout my journey. But for the first time ever, I began to see my life up until that point, as inspirational. My story was different...told from a different vantage point. Sure I had a story, but the story never ended in failure. It continued with me getting back up, wiping the dirt off, and trying again. This reflection and acknowledgment created my fire, and my fire **gave** me motivation. A type of motivation that no one else could **give** me and at that moment, my experiences - all of my experiences - set me on fire.

When you look back over your life, let it inspire you.

Let your experiences set you on fire.

Take Your Seat…

- ***I fell in love with exploration:*** With this newfound motivation, I knew that as long as I put in the work, I could create anything "I put my mind to." Have you ever been told that you "could achieve anything you put your mind to?" Did you believe it at the time? Well, it's true, as we now know that what we tell ourselves we are, whatever we believe, we act upon and that dictates our future. So, I began to explore all the things I was passionate about. I began to look for ways in which I could **give** more meaning to my family, my work, everything and anything I touched. By exploring, I wasn't waiting for growth; I was creating it. You have this same power. The power to explore the deepest parts of who you are, acknowledge what you have discovered, and explore how you can bring them to life.

Take Your Seat…

I fell in love with the work…

- ***Hard, but worth every second, minute, hour:*** There are many terms for this sudden infatuation for creating. Some call it falling in love with the 'chase', others, falling in love with the 'hustle.' However you term it, I fell in love with working on myself and learning everything I could about the world around me.

The more knowledge I sought, the more tools I had to create with. I began to use these tools daily and it entirely transformed my output. The time I was investing created predictable outcomes; outcomes I desired. We'll discuss this more, but for now, I want you to know that changing your mindset is only the beginning. Doing the work has to become an approach; it has to become a behavior; it has to become your way of life.

Every second, every minute, every hour you spend putting in the work is worth it and the return becomes undeniable. You may be asking yourself at this moment, do I have the time? Yes, tell yourself you have the time because what we say, we believe and what we believe, we act upon.

Take your seat…

- *I recommitted to learning:* As a little girl, I was always curious. Often daydreaming about how things worked. I'd ask tons of questions and found myself challenging the first answer I got back. I always wanted to know the other side of the coin but as I grew older, my curiosity became almost obsolete, and I found that it had become easier to take the first answer. Where had my' challenge the status quo' gone? I had put it away nicely in a box.

Funny, how we can lose parts of ourselves when we choose to focus on the negative labels we've prioritized. It felt good to call upon my curiosity once again, and I recommitted myself to learning, for as long as I am here on this earth. That's the beautiful thing about this journey. You may have lost pieces of you along the way, but when you decide that all of you matters and start seeking to know yourself, those things you may have filed away, resurface. Take them back and what…? That's right. *Take your seat…*

Questions to activate an Open mindset

Before we move on, below, I share questions that helped me activate my **Open** mindset:

- *What work can I put in to create desired outcomes?*

- *Do I have a big picture?*

- *Is there more to learn?*

- *Where can I get real constructive feedback?*

- *How do I get to where I desire to go?*

- *What goals can I set to help me reach where I desire to go?*

What you have learned…

- *You deserve to be here, to take your seat at not just this table, but at any table*

- *Words matter*

- *Mindset matters*

- *Failure is a part of the journey*

- *Your life is a point of inspiration*

- *You must do the work*

- *You must be committed to learning*

Take your seat...

CHAPTER 2

WHERE I BELONG

With my new mindset, I stood tall; inspired, driven, and excited. I was **open** and committed to applying this newfound, transcended state to my entire life. Not just at home, not just at work, but in everything I did. It was life-changing.

"How?" Imagine that your whole life up until that point had been decided by what you thought you could not do. And suddenly what you could not do didn't matter. Your life was now focused on the things that you can and would do. That became your vantage point. You saw the world, your life, your work as a canvas. In your hand, you held your paintbrush. By your side, your paint - everything you've gained from **all** of your experiences.

Go ahead...look to your side for just a moment and imagine all that you have...some with the caps on, hidden, compartmentalized, and some with the caps off, those things you've accepted. Look at them; see their value. And from this vantage point, you begin to create... to paint. It did not matter where you started on your canvas, but the more you dipped your brush into **your** paint and took the simple step of bringing **your** brush to canvas, the more **you** created.

The more you created, the more confidence you developed. The more confidence you developed, the more you believed in who you were. You began to trust the notion that as long as you tried, as long as you painted, you would grow - *failure redefined.*

Yes, my life had indeed changed; by simply surrendering and trusting the process. The more I created, the more tangible my creations became. I began to see purpose in the smallest of acts, and I began to see the purpose of my life. All of it, everything I had been through, and it meant something. To think, that what I had been chasing, what seemed like my whole life, was right in front of me.

For the very first time, I knew exactly who I was and what I had next to me, my tools. All that I felt words cannot describe, but I will never forget it. Everything, my whole life, had meaning. And in that moment of clarity, I knew that my life could never be the same.

That was my "call" to greatness. That voice that we hear when we feel inspired, unexpectedly. You see, I had listened to my "call" and had simply taken the step to change my mindset. And in changing my mindset, I was given a blank canvas for creativity. No, I did not have all the answers. I did not know what my canvas would look like when I finished. But I was committed to listening to my "call," and with every stroke, I created the **what**, and I uncovered the **why**.

You see, understanding your purpose doesn't mean you have it all figured out. I was still at the beginning. And I will tell you, your canvas, your story, will never, ever be over until your time here on earth is up. You must understand that your journey will be continuous, you will forever have the power to paint, to create, to make your mark here on earth.

And like a child in a candy store, I painted. I created. And the more I created, the more I impacted others. And just like that, others could feel my authentic desire to **give**. And naturally, they came to expect what I desired to **give.** And yes, I wanted to **give** it, more than anything, I wanted to **give**. It was my commitment, but the fear that came over me, suddenly, was one I could not have prepared for, and I found my mindset in an unexpected war with itself. I questioned if I was the right person...if I was capable of creating anything else. My rides home, sometimes, were episodes of blasting the music to drown out my doubt. Other times, I cried because I felt that I did not deserve what was in me, the fire that burned to inspire others. Can you imagine? All my life I sought this fire, this understanding, and now that I had let it out, I wanted to **box** it back in.

Why? Why on earth would I be afraid of who I was becoming?

Imposter Syndrome
In this chapter, we will dive into "Imposter Syndrome"... what it is, and how you can overcome it.

What is Imposter Syndrome?
Initially, this war that I was in was hard for me to understand, because I knew that I had formed these new beliefs. I believed that I was **open** instead of boxed in, but yet I still found myself here? Although, this time, it was different. "How?" It was different because I knew better. I knew that I could overcome negative labels if I just trusted, if I just listened to my "call"... if I just allowed my fire to comfort me.

When you create, it is your hands that must pick up your brush, and that at times can feel lonely, even if you have amazing people surrounding you, telling you that you can do it. I had to remind myself that if I didn't believe, even when I felt afraid, that it was up to me to keep going and keep painting. The term for this war is Imposter Syndrome.

Imposter Syndrome can happen to anyone at any time. No one is immune. Defined as *a feeling of not being good enough or seeing yourself as a fraud,* these are labels sparked by fear. But like many other labels we give ourselves, they are simply not true.

Your passions, all that you desire to create, all that you were born to create, would not be in you if they were not meant to come from you. I trust that in my life, and you must trust that in yours.

Learn How to Recognize Imposter Syndrome

We know that Imposter Syndrome can happen quite unexpectedly. When it hits, it's best to recognize it for what it is and leverage your new mindset to continue on despite it.

If you find yourself thinking or asking these questions, continue on despite them:

- *There are others who can do this; what could I possibly bring, that's different?*

    ◦ *"You"*

- *What am I really doing here?*

    ◦ *"You were born to be here."*

- *I don't deserve this recognition.*

    - *"Yes, you do. Recognition is a form of gratitude. It's an opportunity for others to say thank you and for you to be thankful for the opportunity to create and effect positive changes on others."*

- *What have I really achieved?*

    - *"What you were born to achieve."*

"She was unstoppable, not because she did not have failures or doubts, but because she continued on despite them." - Beau Taplin

Continue on Despite...

What does it mean to continue on despite...?

It means that this time around, you're not entering into war without your tools. It means that when you fall, you know, you believe, that the only thing to do is to get back up, dust yourself off, and run faster towards your passions. It's understanding that what matters most is not what you can't do, but what you can. It's you believing in yourself, even if fear tells you not to, and even when others doubt you, you choose to continue on. You expect trials, you expect difficult times, but this time, you know that your purpose is bigger than any failure that's ahead of you.

If this sounds easier said than done… You're right because continuing on despite requires grit, girt that you can only get from the ups and downs. It's not a single failure; it's multiple. It's why you hear successful people say; "You've got to get out there and fail, fail hard, because the more you fail, the more you learn, and the more you win." It's a muscle that you have to develop over time.

Below I share ways in which you can strengthen this muscle again and again until it becomes second nature.

- *Recognize Imposter Syndrome Quickly & Respond Just as Quick:* A negative thought will always be a negative thought. As quick as it comes into your space, tell yourself just as quick, negativity at this point in your life, has no truth.

Take your seat, Continue on despite...

- *Authentic Acknowledgment:* Others **will** notice your fire. Some will feel your fire, and others may simply come to watch. Be comfortable with being your authentic self and acknowledging that you don't know what your canvas will look like when your time is up, but whatever it ends up being, you will be its author. That alone is enough to keep going; to keep painting while not having all of the answers.

Take your seat, Continue on despite...

- *Share:* Here is where vulnerability will win over hiding who you are becoming. In coaching, I'd tell you; you've hidden for far too long. You're here; there is no turning back. Once I turned myself on, once my fire was lit, I knew I could never turn it off. So, when those negative thoughts come, share, be vulnerable with someone you trust, and get those thoughts out of your head. And the conversation goes something like this... "I don't think I can do this. What? Are you serious? Do you know how amazing you are? How much you've touched others? Come on; you've got this." Ever heard that before?

Take your seat, Continue on despite...

- **Reframe your thoughts:** Words will continue to be powerful. If you are experiencing negative thoughts and feel stuck, try reframing them and take a different position. For example, if I found myself feeling inadequate, I would reframe my thoughts and tell myself, "the fact that I am feeling inadequate right now, doesn't mean that I am."

Take your seat, Continue on despite...

- **Be kind to yourself:** You won't have all the answers, and that's okay. If you fail, you know now, that the world will not end. You will grow. But if you accomplish something that challenged you, made you sweat...treat yourself. It doesn't have to be big; it could be a positive affirmation, a celebration of a new tool by sharing how you overcame a challenge and how you solved it, and how you painted it.

Take your seat, Continue on despite...

- **Seek Support:** Everyone needs support, someone in their corner rooting them on. I liken this to what a coach is to their athletes, what parents are to their children, what a spouse is to their wife or husband. You must have mentors, coaches that will always see greatness in you, that will always acknowledge your potential, that will always tell you the truth so that you strive continuously to be better. You deserve this type of support.

Take your seat, Continue on despite...

Imposter Syndrome; A Good Thing?

Yes. Have you ever been told that "if it doesn't scare you, you aren't dreaming big enough?" Here's why...

- *Fear Showed Me:* Fear has always been my greatest compass. It showed me exactly where to go. Think about it, the times you were afraid to step out and try something new, and you mustered up enough courage to do it, and enjoyed it! The same thing, fear is your whole being saying this is unfamiliar. I don't know how this is going to turn out and so let's not do this. Absolutely not. *Failure redefined,* and more.

Take your seat, Continue on despite...

- *Feet on the ground:* Whether you're nervous about presenting your idea, speaking up on a companywide call, or stepping out on your own as an entrepreneur, fear makes you human. It keeps you humble and keeps your feet on the ground.

Take your seat, Continue on despite...

What I learned...

- There are different faces of the Imposter Syndrome. It's good to know the differences, so you are better equipped to recognize them faster and take action.

1. The Perfectionist

Imposter Syndrome and perfectionism, normally go hand-in-hand. Perfectionists are known to set extremely high goals, and when they experience setbacks, they immediately feel they are incapable. Once a perfectionist feels incapable, they feel they have lost control, and they do not see how the task can ever be completed if it's not perfect. You must understand that failure is part of your growth.

Are you a perfectionist?

- *Do you think perfection is attainable?*

- *Do you believe that anything below perfection is not worth giving to the world?*

If you answered yes to either question, I must say that there is no such thing as perfection. There is only your best. Just like technology changes and evolves, there is always a way to do it better. What matters most is that you **gave** your best here and now, and then believe that your best has a purpose. Your best has meaning.

And with purpose and meaning, you can **give** your creativity to the world, not when it's perfect, but when it's your best.

Take your seat, Continue on despite...

2. The Superman/woman

With this type of Imposter Syndrome, you feel somewhat invincible, as though you are made of Teflon and are somehow superhuman. You push yourself until you are drained. Here is where I would say as a coach, it's important to not only listen to your "call" but also listen to your physical self. Your body knows when it's time to take a break and recharge so that you can come back stronger.

Are you superhuman? :

- *Does your health take a backseat to everything else?*

- *Despite your achievements, do you feel you haven't done enough?*

- *Do you feel validation when others recognize your work?*

A yes to any of these questions gets the same response. Your life matters, and if you are not here to create, your mark can't be made. The only validation that your life requires is the validation you get when you wake with each morning. Nothing else matters when it comes to your existence. Your health must be a priority.

Knowing where your validation comes from is critical. Whatever name you **give** your creator, the breath in your body **gives** wind to your creativity. Take care of yourself. You deserve that.

Take your seat, Continue on despite...

3. The Natural Genius

Ironically people with this Imposter Syndrome judge their competence based on the speed and ease of their work, as opposed to the sweat and tears they are putting in. They find themselves feeling shame and inadequacy, the longer it takes to master or accomplish something.

Although external factors do not really affect them that much, they normally set their internal bar pretty high. You can judge yourself extremely hard if you fall short.

Are you the Natural Genius?

- *Do you have to be the "smartest person in the room?"*

- *Do you avoid what you perceive as difficult?*

- *When you fail, do you feel shame?*

We are all works in progress. We know our journeys are continuous. We should never stop learning because when we stop learning, we stop growing. It's okay not to know everything, that's what makes our journey so special.

Take your seat, Continue on despite...

4. The Soloist

Those in this category feel weak in some capacity if they ask for help. Instead, they decide to go at it alone, putting themselves in jeopardy of stalling their growth.

Are you a Soloist?

- *Do you believe you have to run your race alone?*

- *Do you believe you can do it by yourself?*

- *Do you believe there is no one to help you ?*

There is not one person on this planet who doesn't need help with something. Ask for help if you need it. You will grow in the process.

Take your seat, Continue on despite...

5. The Expert

This type of Imposter Syndrome ties competence to 'what' and 'how much' is done and known. There is a fear that you will never know enough and get exposed as un-knowledgeable or inexperienced.

Are you an Expert?

- *Do you compare yourself to a checklist?*

- *Do certifications define your ability to be successful?*

- *Do you constantly doubt your acumen?*

Learning is important, but must not impede upon your practice time. What good is a play if it's never run through on the field? Here is where taking risks and trusting in yourself become important.

Now you may be asking, "Christine, which one of these Imposter Syndromes have you experienced?" I've experienced all of them at different points in my journey, but I continue(d) on despite them. You have that power too.

Take your seat, Continue on despite..

CHAPTER 3

CONFIDENCE NEVER
FELT SO GOOD

Inhale (1,2,3,4,5)...now exhale (1,2,3,4,5)... Inhale (1,2,3,4,5)...now exhale (1,2,3,4,5)... Inhale (1,2,3,4,5)...now exhale (1,2,3,4,5)... How did that feel?

It's like finally having space in your life to "stop and smell the roses." Finally, life has created a safe space for you to take your breaths, above water. It's unconstricted and liberating. You're no longer drowning in a box full of negative labels and inaction. Go ahead, do it again. Inhale (1,2,3,4,5)...now exhale (1,2,3,4,5)...Inhale (1,2,3,4,5)...now exhale (1,2,3,4,5)... Inhale (1,2,3,4,5)...now exhale (1,2,3,4,5)... That breath just feels so good. It is the confidence in who you are; the confidence in your belief that you are capable, so much more capable, of creating the rest of your life and exploring all the possibilities that are ahead.

It is here. You've heard your "call" to greatness, and you believe that you **do** have a purpose; to create. But with this new confidence, this sense of self, how do you remain humble? How do you embrace your fire and keep your feet on the ground?

My journey up until this point has stirred up so many emotions. First, gratitude for my peace of mind, I could think differently. Excitement, for my desire to paint, I could create. Happiness, for my sense of identity, I could tell you exactly who I was. I felt confident, and it was an emotion I wanted to embrace. Now that I had it, I didn't want to let it go. I didn't want to turn off my fire, **ever**. But how would my fire affect those around me?

In this chapter, we will dive into embracing who you are while leveraging emotional intelligence to remain humble but firm in your newfound confidence.

The Embrace
Who are you?

A question, at one point, I could not answer. But now, if you asked me, even if I didn't have the answer fully baked, I could go back. I could reference my canvas. I could see every stroke, and I could tell you every color, the genesis of my impact. Owner of every can of paint that lay by my side.

And the more I painted, the more work I did on my canvas, the more I could define it. I could give it a name. Clarity, in its most authentic form. I was me, and the "me" was transforming every day. I had embraced the idea that life as I knew it did not exist within the walls I once boxed myself in, but my life could be whatever I created on the canvas, an infinite form of expression.

Yes, I felt confident, and that confidence never felt so good. For the first time, my fire had consumed all of me. I had completely embraced my flame. Wherever it led me, I would go. That is and will always be my commitment, the substance of my authenticity.

So what do you do? How do people respond when you have become consumed by your own fire?

What is Emotional Intelligence?

At its core, it is the ability to be empathic. It is the authentic desire to appreciate humanity in its purest form. To understand one's own emotions and the emotions of others in such a way that through interaction, meaningful connections are made. An individual with emotional intelligence, can leverage what they have gained from their connections and then use that insight as a guide to drive outcomes and leave lasting impressions.

At this point in my journey, I had to understand that living out of the box came with a responsibility, not only to myself, but to others. Let's look at how I exercise that responsibility first, to others, and then to myself.

Self-awareness

Moments of introspection are powerful. They provide an opportunity to assess one's own emotional and mental state. It is being self-aware of the effect your flame is having on others around you. As more and more people drew closer to me, I had to understand the impact I would have on others and my intentions. I had to be self-aware of how I came into the interaction, how I connected, and how

I responded. This is not something I learned overnight. It is something I could only begin to understand through practice. Here, I share ways in which I continue to strengthen this muscle.

- **Be Present:** What does it mean to be present? Being present requires you to be emotionally vested in the moment. To be emotionally vested in the moment, you've got to know how you are showing up. That means when I have the opportunity to interact with someone in whatever capacity that is required for me to interact with that person, I have to be aware of what emotions I'm bringing to that interaction.

  I'll give you an example. If I am due to be in a meeting in the next ten minutes, and the team has just handed me down bad news on another item, for me to have meaningful interaction in that meeting, I can't bring in what I feel about the bad news. I have to *continue on despite*. Sound familiar?

  What I came to realize, was that my own emotions could become distractions if I allowed them to be. That if I was going to serve others and remain humble, I had to be present by removing emotions that did not serve those I interacted with.

Take your seat, Continue on despite, Remain humble...

Emotional Appreciation: To understand what emotions would and would not serve others, I had to establish what I call 'Emotional Appreciation.' What do I mean by that? I had to learn the value of the emotions I carried at any **given** time. I had to establish a certain appreciation for emotions by considering how they would affect others.

In the example above, it would not have served those in the meeting if I had brought the emotion of disappointment along. What would my behavior have been if I showed up already disappointed? What weight would I have **given** the dialogue of those participating? It is critical that as your fire grows, you always remain aware of the value that your emotions **give** at any time. If it does not serve those you connect with, leave them at the door.

Take your seat, Continue on despite, Remain humble...

- **The Response:**

  Just like I had to exercise emotional appreciation for my emotions, I also had to learn how to do the same for others. You see, as your flame grows, there may be others that become uncomfortable with your confidence, with your fire. So, what do you do? Do you respond? And if so, how do you respond?

  I will level set and say, restraint is one of the most powerful responses you can **give**. It is better not to respond. But if you do respond, it is important to have an appreciation for the emotion of the other person, meaning their emotion is not your emotion. It is theirs and theirs alone.

I wish I could tell you that the more you paint and run towards your purpose, everyone will love this newfound you; but I can't, because they won't. Those that are meant to be transformed by your fire, **will**, but you also have to be cognizant of the other crowd that you will draw. You've got to know that part of being emotionally intelligent is the ability to rise above any emotion that creates negative feelings in you.

If you've just said, "That's hard to do, Christine," remember how powerful labels are. You are capable of rising above anything that doesn't serve you.

Take your seat, Continue on despite, Remain humble...

Emotional Channeling

- *Stand in power:* Let's dive into your ability to rise above a little further. If someone does behave in a way that makes you feel negative or bad, what do you do with that negativity? Learning how to channel your emotions becomes critical. As human beings, we are designed to feel emotion, and so it is normal to feel bad if someone has hurt you. But what do you do with that hurt? Do you **give** back what you've just been **given**, or do you channel your emotions and **give** something different? How you choose to react to that hurt, determines whether or not you allow others' emotions to snuff out your fire. No negative emotion has to be met with more negative emotion.

Psychologists call this emotional channeling, 'goal-directed behavior.' Instead of returning negative emotions you've just been given, channel your emotions in a way that aligns with the goal that you are looking to achieve with that person. No one should be able to move you out of your character.

*In any situation, it is you who has the power to choose who you will be in that moment. Stand in your power **always**.*

Take your seat, Continue on despite, Remain humble...

Let's take a small shift now towards the responsibility we have towards ourselves to remain humble in our consuming fire and pursuit; what

I call 'behind the scenes work.' I shared earlier that our journeys are never over; they are continuous. We should never get to a point where we feel we've learned all there is to learn. Here, I share how I exercise humility within my exploration.

Emotions; a Source of Self-Motivation

- *I return to my canvas:* Have you ever completely lost yourself in something that brought you joy, something you were really excited to do? You look around, and you are three hours into what you were doing and feel it's only been a few minutes.

"Time flies when you are having fun."

This is me when I have set aside time to create. Time seems to have no limit, and I become immersed in the act of creating what could be. The feeling that comes over me as I go deeper, as I explore the unknown, is freedom. Freedom to create all that I will **give**. That feeling of freedom motivates me to keep going. To keep returning to my canvas, to prioritize my creativity time.

I humbly commit to sit at my canvas and create, because I know there is still more for me to learn and understand. And once I'm there at my canvas, all of the emotions I feel that come with putting my paintbrush to the canvas, become all the motivation I need to keep going.

Even if I don't feel like creating, I know that if I just go to my canvas, taking that action will motivate me to keep going. You have to trust that, always.

There will be days when you don't feel motivated to create and work towards your purpose. There will be times when you feel you have learned all that you can learn or created all that you can create. You must remain humble and commit to going to your canvas, always.

Take your seat, Continue on despite, Remain humble...

Humbly Confident

When you reference the word 'humble,' you'll find several words that appear to be the complete opposite of 'confident.' Some people see humility as a strength, and others as a weakness. Quite the conundrum, when you think about how the two can live within the same space. How do we stand firm in who we are, always, and remain humble at the same time?

Just like your commitment to go to your canvas, so must you commit to practicing humble confidence. Below, I share ways in which I embrace both.

Take your seat, Continue on despite, Remain humble...

Remain open to feedback

Humility requires an honest assessment of our impact. To remain humble, I allow others to speak into my life. I practice **giving** them a safe space to give their opinions. I remain open to feedback and criticism.

Remember, people should always be entitled to their opinion, and I trust that I will know if the feedback is genuine. I can take what is helpful and leave behind the rest, but I have to be comfortable with getting feedback so that I can take those corrective steps and become better. Being humbly confident means you remain coachable throughout your journey. It is something you must seek.

Take your seat, Continue on despite, Remain humble...

It's Bigger

Your purpose will always be bigger than who you are becoming. What you create, what you **give** to the world, will never be about you. I remind myself of this daily. This awareness allows me to keep my feet planted firmly on the ground. I was born to serve others. That is our purpose.

Being humbly confident is always knowing that it's not about you, it's not about who sees you, it's not about who praises you. It will always be about how your fire impacts others, your legacy.

Take your seat, Continue on despite, Remain humble...

Practice Gratitude

So many people have helped me get to this point in my life. For them, I will always be thankful. To those that pushed me past my own fears, I will always be thankful. To those that told me I could not, and I would not, for them, I will always be thankful. To those that doubted me more than I doubted myself, I will always be thankful to you. To those that wanted me to fail, I failed, and I am so thankful that I did. It allowed me to *redefine my failure* and helped me grow into the person I am now. Thank you.

You see, everything you've experienced up until this point has made you who you are today. I would never go back and ask to do it all over again. When you embrace your journey, you let go of regrets. Be thankful for everything you've been through so that you can be thankful for where you are going. To be humbly confident, you've got to be thankful for it **all**.

Take your seat, Continue on despite, Remain humble...

Check the Other Side

As you create, you will begin to master your work, but as we discussed earlier, you will never be done learning. . In your journey, you will come to understand that there is always another way of doing it. There is always the other side of the coin.

Being humbly confident means that you are **open** to checking the other side; to learning if there are better ways to create. You remain firm in what you are seeking to create, but **open** to other ways in which you can accomplish your desired outcome.

Take your seat, Continue on despite, Remain humble...

Take Leaps of Faith

Creating without knowing where you will end up is nothing short of a leap. In your humility, you've got to know that you may get it wrong. You may fail at it. But in your confidence, you know at this point, a leap and miss is not a miss at all. Here is where I say; you've got to get comfortable with taking risks.

Being humbly confident means that you are willing to roll with punches; to accept that this pursuit will not be easy. That you will be faced with challenges. You will get it right, and you will get it wrong, but through it all, you know that every piece of your journey will continue to have purpose and meaning. Trust this always.

Take your seat, Continue on despite, Remain humble...

Run towards Possibility

Once you've taken the leap, you've got to run towards possibility. That means you can't leap and then tiptoe towards what's possible. Remember, there is nothing you can't accomplish once you've put your mind to it. What is possible can only be proven by testing it.

Being humbly confident means that you are willing to test your creativity so that what you are destined to **give,** can reach more people. Similar to checking the other side, possibilities demonstrate opportunity. We have to know that the world **gives** us unlimited possibilities to explore. Never be afraid to explore the possibilities.

Take your seat, Continue on despite, Remain humble...

CHAPTER 4

HELLO HABITS!

Here is where I would ask; "What do you believe **now**? What are you capable of **now**? **Now** that you've been set on fire, what will keep you going? Will you **always** listen to that voice, your 'call?' When you are faced with doubt, will you *continue on despite…*?

Through my journey, I've gotten pretty familiar with these questions. They are questions I ask myself often. Self-driven accountability, to help me understand what it is, I truly believe. When I am challenged, do I **give** up… or do I find strength in my beliefs? When I've **given** all that I can to my creativity, will I, in that moment of seeming 'exhaustion', still believe that there is more that I can **give**?

What do I believe, right **now**?

I believe that once you've been set on fire, you would have experienced the greatest transformation of your existence; in complete alignment with the 'why' you were put on this earth. A question you have sought an answer to for most of your life. It's been in your curiosity, in your daydreams, in your smiles, and yes, even in your pain. Your whole life has had meaning and purpose. But will that be enough to keep **you** going?

Do you believe that once you have found your purpose, your journey gets easier? That you will always feel motivated to keep going? What will sustain your fire?

In this chapter, we say hello to habits, as we lay the foundation for consistency and discipline.

First, let's look at habits and how they are formed.

Habits; How They Work

A habit in itself is comprised of three components: *a cue, a routine,* and *a reward.* This means, our habits are cued by triggers and once triggered, we behave in a routine to the point our behavior becomes automatic. Why? Because we get pleasure from that behavior; positive reinforcement for us to do it again and again.

I will make the distinction here, that there are good habits that drive desired outcomes, and then there are habits that simply do not serve our purpose. Yet, we gain pleasure from both. If we gain pleasure from both, why would we ever want to get rid of habits that do not serve the future we are creating? The better question is, why would we not?

Here, is where I acknowledge that you will indeed find many people who will tell you, it is too difficult to break bad habits. But you see, that can't be a label we give ourselves, because if we do, we will never remove those things that do not serve our purpose.

In my journey, here's what I learned about removing habits and creating a healthy space for new habits to form...

Redirect Your Focus

How do you feel when you focus on those things that you've identified as negative in your life? Negative, right? Same thing, here. What I learned was that if I wanted to get rid of those habits that did not serve my purpose and where I felt called to go, it did me no good to focus on them. So, I began to redirect my focus towards creating new habits. Habits I needed, to establish consistency and discipline around my creativity.

And as I began to create new habits, those habits began to establish new 'routines' in my life. They became part of my daily practice and eventually consumed those habits that didn't serve my purpose. I had no room left for the ones that did not align with who I had become. My new habits gave me discipline and created a framework for my life. And similar to 'the more I painted, the more I created', the more I formed new habits that aligned with my purpose, the more tangible my purpose became. The who I was to become, began to take form. Some may call this 'manifestation.' I call it, **doing the work**.

What I've just shared with you is the blueprint for creating the rest of your life. Results are in your habits. Outcomes are in your habits. Change rest in your habits. Your ability to fulfil your unique purpose comes down to your habits. Create habits that serve your purpose, and you will become consistently disciplined in what you desire and are meant to **give**.

So going forward, we will focus on creating new habits that serve your purpose and are in complete alignment with the mark that you are destined to make.

Become and Remain Committed

Research suggests that habits are formed over time. They do not appear out of thin air. So, if I was going to focus on creating new habits, I knew I also had to be committed over time. Leveraging what I knew about mindset, I gave myself the label of commitment, and I became committed to the process. I knew that as long as I committed to the right behaviors, they would eventually become automatic.

And they did.

No magic tricks here, simply, the power of my beliefs allowed me to create habits that aligned with where I wanted to go and who I wanted to be.

Take your seat, Continue on despite, Remain humble, Align your habits...

Explore

We looked at exploration earlier, where we discussed exploring our passions and who we were becoming. Exploration is also relevant here. There has to be an exploration; a discovery process. Allow yourself the opportunity to explore how to incorporate that habit into your life.

In the process, I discovered I was more creative at night after I had put the kids to bed. When I'm developing a strategy, or I'm in 'planning mode', I have more clarity when I listen to music. I like to exercise in the evening rather than in the morning. All of these things make me who I am. An added benefit that comes with you creating habits that serve your purpose is that you become more in tune with who you are. And the more you know about yourself, the more you can **give**. When you set off to create new habits, you'll have to discover the best way to weave these habits into your daily practice.

Take your seat, Continue on despite, Remain humble, Align your habits...

Continue To Build

As you implement these new habits into your life, don't stop. Keep going. Continue to build upon all that you are gaining from the change that you see in your life. Your change will become tangible. Run towards that change. The more I ran towards change, the more disciplined I became. The more focused I was and the more I could create routinely.

Build upon who you are by forming good habits and become more equipped to **give**. Never stop building, make it a lifestyle.

Take your seat, Continue on despite, Remain humble, Align your habits...

Enjoy the Journey

As new habits are created in your life, and your life begins to change as a result of these habits, joy and fulfilment are natural results of the work you are doing. I have gained so much fulfilment from just doing the work. You've got to fall in love with this part of your evolution. Enjoy the journey, enjoy the grind, enjoy the exploration, my friend.

Take your seat, Continue on despite, Remain humble, Align your habits...

Stay Focused on the Big Picture

If you're asking yourself, what happens if I have a bad day? What happens if there are days I don't create? Those days will happen, but they do not define you. What matters is what you believe in that moment.

Yes, I have had tough days, and despite those tough days, I had to trust the process and stay focused on the big picture. Reminding myself that failure in a moment didn't define the entire journey. If you have a bad day, you've got to stay focused on the big picture, your purpose.

And if you're saying Christine, "Consistency is one of my weaknesses."

Before we close this chapter, I'll share a few tips that can help you build up that consistency.

Take your seat, Continue on despite, Remain humble, Align your habits...

Occasional Breaks

I trust that you know how you work best. If you burn out easily and that burnout depletes your motivation, treat yourself to an occasional break. Remember, habits are formed over time. Eventually, your efforts will pay off. If you feel that you need a break, listen to your body and set a day aside for self-care, rest, relaxation, or whatever your heart desires. Allow your recharge to **give** you the strength you need to keep going.

Take your seat, Continue on despite, Remain humble, Align your habits...

Switch Things Up

What happens if your routine no longer fits into your daily practice? You continued to evolve on your journey and what worked before, no longer fits into your schedule. **Give** yourself permission to switch things up and do it differently. As long as you are **giving** it your best, that is all that matters.

Take your seat, Continue on despite, Remain humble, Align your habits...

External Accountability

Whether a coach, mentor, friend, family member or colleague, it is important that you have someone in your life to hold you accountable. And not just to hold you accountable, but to also listen to you. To hear everything good in your life, but also your challenges. Someone comfortable being in both of these moments with you and can provide you with the insight you need to keep going.

Take your seat, Continue on despite, Remain humble, Align your habits...

Celebrate

Learn to celebrate the change(s) that you see in your life. This doesn't always mean that you should throw yourself a party. Perhaps, the simple act of acknowledging that you've created change in your life. That acknowledgement could be writing it down in your journal or sharing it with someone important to you. Either way, you have acknowledged the change and can tie it directly to the new behaviors you have formed.

Take your seat, Continue on despite, Remain humble, Align your habits...

CHAPTER 5

DO YOU SEE IT?

Your **embrace**…

It is my desire that as you read this book, you truly see how your experiences **have** made you special. That you rip off any negative labels you have attached to who you are. That you understand; even when you don't believe in yourself …when others don't believe in who you are becoming, that you wouldn't be here if you were not meant to spend the rest of your life creating, painting your canvas, and understanding the value you have to **give**.

Be with me in this moment. A space of vulnerability. A willingness to set your sights towards the unknown. This isn't just a book you are reading; this is a message that was created for you, for this moment. An opportunity for you to truly look within and realize that yes… you **are** the only person on earth that can leave your **unique** mark.

You have the power to embrace all of who you are. You have the power to embrace all that you have to **give**; your fire. And even if your answer is not fully baked, you can see exactly what is next to you, what is inside of you, the strokes of your own paintbrush. And even if your canvas is blank right now, even if you'd say... "Christine, I've not yet started..." that you realize that a blank canvas, even in this moment, means that you're right where you are supposed to be, wanting, yearning for more to **give**.

Be with me in this moment. Where is your flame? What in your life is waiting to set you on fire? Never to be boxed in again, what is waiting to move you towards your purpose so that you can live life unapologetically **open**?

Be with me in this moment. What is it that makes you most afraid? What have you always wanted to pursue, but did not?

Be with me in this moment. How do you move forward, knowing that every single human being has lived a life of preparation, not to be disqualified by failure but as a demonstration of their transformative strength?

DO YOU SEE IT?

It is **you**. It has always been you. **Discovery**; it starts with you. **Change**; it starts with you. **Impact**; it starts with you. The **mark** you'll leave can only start with you. And I'm so happy it's you. Because there is no one else. No one else that can do what you were designed to do.

So, you owe it to yourself and to the world to **believe**...

Take your seat, Continue on despite, Remain humble, Align your habits, Believe & know your value...

No matter what...believe...No matter how hard it gets...believe... No matter how many times you fall down...believe...No matter the amount of times you have to get back up and dust yourself off...believe...No matter your doubts in this moment or the next... believe...Even when you feel you've **given** all that you can **give**, that you've created all that you can create, in that moment... **you must believe.**

This is how you light your fire and keep it burning. This is how you must live for the rest of your life... Believing in all that you are and are destined to be.

Take your seat, Continue on despite, Remain humble, Align your habits, Believe & know your value...

Inhale (1,2,3,4,5)... Exhale (1,2,3,4,5)...Inhale (1,2,3,4,5)...Exhale (1,2,3,4,5).

That's it...Take your breaths above water, my friend... Because you'll never have to turn back from this point. You'll never have to see your life as just happening to you, but that for the rest of your life, you will happen to the world.

Take your seat, Continue on despite, Remain humble, Align your habits, Believe & know your value...

Stay right here...In this moment of reflection and self-awareness.

In this chapter, we dive deeper into self-awareness and how it helps you see yourself for all that you will **give**; your value.

To Be Self-Aware...

Is to be Enlightened

You may refer to your clarity in this moment, as having more understanding, more insight, or more awakening, but they are all forms of enlightenment. The truth is, you are now equipped to think differently, completely aware of how change is forged, how impact is made, and how intricate your involvement is, in all that you create. Your awareness affords you not only confidence, but a life lived from a position of power. The power to create the most extraordinary outcomes. Outcomes that will shake the world.

DO YOU SEE IT?

Take your seat, Continue on despite, Remain humble, Align your habits, Believe & know your value...

Is to be Disciplined

Discipline will not only emerge from your habits but will also create them in the future. The power to instill discipline in every facet of your existence; to control your time, your energy, what you eat, and when you sleep; a gradual evolution of how you exist within each day.

DO YOU SEE IT?

Take your seat, Continue on despite, Remain humble, Align your habits, Believe & know your value...

Is to be Excellent

Excellence is not perfection. Excellence is the relentless pursuit to always **give** your best, those things that make you great, the journey towards perfection. To never settle or be compromised. To understand that right is right and wrong is wrong and then choose to always stand for what is right.

To *continue on despite*. To take the road less traveled because your beliefs outweigh the risks. Excellence is being aware that your only option is to run towards what you stand for, even in the absence of validation from others.

DO YOU SEE IT?

Take your seat, Continue on despite, Remain humble, Align your habits, Believe & know your value...

Is to be Unshaken

Unshakeable in your beliefs, you live a life of conviction. Your standards and morals precede you. When you are tested, challenged, or provoked, you are unmoved. You are fully aware that someone else's biased perceptions or beliefs do not define who you are or what you'll become. You stand firm.

DO YOU SEE IT?

Take your seat, Continue on despite, Remain humble, Align your habits, Believe & know your value...

Is to be Aligned

You are aligned in all that you do. Your habits are aligned with your goals. Your goals are aligned with your purpose. Your network is aligned with your purpose. Your relationships are aligned with your purpose. Your beliefs remain aligned with your purpose. You are aware that you deserve to live a life of complete alignment.

DO YOU SEE IT?

Take your seat, Continue on despite, Remain humble, Align your habits, Believe & know your value...

All these things combined, with your purpose, create your value.

Know Your Value

Here, I will remind you of your power to believe. This awareness should establish a new set of labels for you. All that you can bring to your purpose, to your creativity, to your family, and to your work.

Strength: Your pain is your inspiration
Mindful: You are aware
Creative: You build freely
Powerful: You are the creator of your life
Courageous: You know exactly what fear means
Established: You have a command on your life
Convicted: You stand firm in your beliefs

Take your seat, Continue on despite, Remain humble, Align your habits, Believe & know your value...

Before we move forward, it is important to acknowledge that your level of awareness will grow over time. And you can contribute to its development. So, let's look at ways to strengthen this particular muscle of awareness.

Prioritize

Yes...you must **give** yourself permission to prioritize this way of living. It is a choice. We will talk more in-depth on this topic, but every day you must choose to live the rest of your life from this level of enlightenment. It must become a priority. And as you evolve into the best version of yourself, fully positioned to **give** and fulfill your purpose in life, it is you who must prioritize who you have become.

Take your seat, Continue on despite, Remain humble, Align your habits, Believe & know your value...

Be Curious

You must always seek answers. You must be willing to understand life in all its complexities. Always seek to know and understand what happens behind the curtain. And even when given an answer, you must be willing to delve deeper. Listen to your gut here, and if you feel there is more to know, more to understand, follow that, unapologetically. Never be ashamed of wanting to know more or to challenge the status quo.

Take your seat, Continue on despite, Remain humble, Align your habits, Believe & know your value...

Be Vulnerable

You're on fire, and being on fire, your authenticity will be felt. **Give** it. The more vulnerable you are with what moves you, the more you provide a safe place for others to **open** up, and the more value you create.

Take your seat, Continue on despite, Remain humble, Align your habits, Believe & know your value...

Strive

Strive to challenge yourself. Become aware of your strengths and where you need improvement. Do the work to improve your understanding of how you respond when you are challenged. Ask for help and guidance on what you do not understand. As you learn, the more you can **give**, and the more value you will bring.

Take your seat, Continue on despite, Remain humble, Align your habits, Believe & know your value...

Write

Write as much as you can. Allow it to be an expressive portal for your thoughts, ideas, dreams, emotions, strengths, weaknesses, realizations, intentions, beliefs, accountability, and creativity.

A safe haven to see what is inside of you at any **given** time in your evolution.

Take your seat, Continue on despite, Remain humble, Align your habits, Believe & know your value...

Be Empathetic

Practice empathy not just for others, but also situational empathy. Be slow to react and become increasingly aware of all that is happening around you, what led to the situation, and how you can best serve in that moment.

Take your seat, Continue on despite, Remain humble, Align your habits, Believe & know your value...

Listen

Hear differently... hearing not only what is being said but also what is not being said. Listen with the intent of understanding. Becoming aware of the beliefs that are influencing what is being spoken. Then and only then should you form words that have an appreciation for what you have heard.

Take your seat, Continue on despite, Remain humble, Align your habits, Believe & know your value...

Expand & Collaborate

As you draw others to you, be aware of how you can expand and grow together. Collaboration, learning together, working together, only increases your awareness. "Two heads **are** better than one."

Take your seat, Continue on despite, Remain humble, Align your habits, Believe & know your value...

Serve

Find ways to serve others through your work and in your community. This mentality exposes you to others' reality, their challenges, their initiatives, their passions, their dreams, and their greatness... Becoming more aware of how to **give**, where you may be needed, and where you can provide support.

Take your seat, Continue on despite, Remain humble, Align your habits, Believe & know your value...

Embrace Wellness

I'd be remiss if I did not share the importance of embracing your complete wellness. The mind, body, and soul all require attention. Whatever you believe in, you must embrace wellness. Embracing wellness requires you to prioritize your overall health. Treat your body well, be aware of what it is telling you, so that you can be most physically effective throughout your journey.

Take your seat, Continue on despite, Remain humble, Align your habits, Believe & know your value...

Acknowledge

Part of knowing what failure truly is requires that you acknowledge when things have not gone as expected, or when you've made a mistake. It's aware of the lessons as you experience them. Learning from events as they unfold and seeking to understand the lessons more clearly.

Take your seat, Continue on despite, Remain humble, Align your habits, Believe & know your value...

These areas of focus will strengthen and transform your awareness, but most importantly, demonstrate your undeniable value. As we close this chapter, I encourage you to apply your value to all that you do. Furthermore, bring all of you; all of these things that comprise your value.

What you have learned...

- *You must believe*

- *You must practice self-awareness so that you understand your value*

- *Your value is comprised of your ability to be fully aware of what you have to give*

- *You can strengthen your awareness by:*

  - *Prioritizing*

  - *Being Curious*

  - *Being Vulnerable*

- *Striving*

- *Writing*

- *Being Empathetic*

- *Listening*

- *Expanding & Collaborating*

- *Serving*

- *Embracing Wellness*

- *Acknowledgment.*

Take your seat, Continue on despite, Remain humble, Align your habits, Believe & Know your value...

CHAPTER 6

NOW THEY SEE IT

Has there ever been that one person? That one person whose presence you felt filling the entire room… Who inspired you to believe that indeed you could accomplish anything that you set out to do… One who made you believe that trying, was always going to be worth it no matter the outcome. Their fearlessness **gave** you courage. They inspired you, not just because of their story, but also how they chose to live the rest of their life. Their fire was contagious…It was consuming…It was unboxed, **open**, and left a lasting impression on you.

It was their **impact**; the legacy they were creating by serving others, that **gave** you hope…hope that change **was** possible, and no matter how many times you'd fallen down up until that point, it was you who held the power to create a life of **greatness**.

Has there……?

You see, at this moment, whether you tell me yes or no, what you must know is that it is YOU who is capable of having that same lasting **impact** on others. And just like the source of pain becomes no measure of your value, the fact that you may not have been told that despite it all, your **greatness** will one day fill a room; that it is you who will leave others feeling that they can accomplish anything they set out to do...that you will demonstrate how trying will always be worth it...that your fearlessness will **give** others the courage to go after all of their dreams...That your fire, the way you choose to live the rest of your life, will **give** hope to others...hope for change, and hope that **greatness**, not perfection, but **greatness,** was always in the cards.

You see, your greatness is and always will be found in the impact you leave on others. They will see it, they will feel it, and they will never forget it. This is the power of your impact. It is the reason you were put on this earth and is what **gives** your life meaning; your purpose.

In this Chapter, I empower you to run towards your purpose, as I share with you this guide to creating impact and the forms it can take.

A Guide to Creating Impact...

Dedicate your time to what gives your life meaning and purpose

What do we do with the time we are given? With the ideas that come to mind? With the things that perhaps inspire us, unexpectedly? Do we take the time to explore, to go deeper? ... Or do we spend our time on things that do not serve our purpose? What response do we **give** to our call?

Do you believe that you can do it later, maybe tomorrow, or have you decided it's too late?

When you are looking to create impact, to leave your mark, and **give** your life meaning and purpose, you've got to know that one of the most valuable assets you possess is time. Your time is precious, and therefore, it becomes critical for you to channel your time towards acts that serve your purpose.

I am often asked, "Christine, how do you find the time to do it all?" My response to that question is; you make time for what you are passionate about...for what is important to you. I remind myself that with every waking morning, I am given another twenty-four hours to take steps that are aligned with my purpose.

There is no secret formula...it's simply got to be important to you. It's got to be what drives you, each and every day. Leaving your mark, doing the work, building, creating, and sacrificing, so that you can serve others, has to be a priority.

Take your seat, Continue on despite, Remain humble, Align your habits, Believe & know your value, Create impact...

Commit to growth; to become better

We know that perfection does not exist... And if perfection does not exist, what is it that we should really strive for? Creating impact requires a commitment to live life knowing that we truly are afforded unlimited possibilities. It's the fork in the road at which we find ourselves, again and again.

We should always strive to be the best we can be, never settling... never thinking that we have reached our pinnacle. We can always do more, we can create more, and most of all, we can learn more. As long as we are **given** time here on earth, we have the opportunity to become better, to continuously reach new heights and then, begin again.

Take your seat, Continue on despite, Remain humble, Align your habits, Believe & know your value, Create impact...

Establish connections through authenticity and alignment

Connections are powerful and go beyond "relationships." To be connected with another human being means, you have a safe space to share ideas, opinions, passions, needs, weaknesses, and strengths. And within that connection lies a genuine appreciation for what makes that person **great**, who they are now, and who they seek to become in the future. It is authenticity, the expression of humanity in its purest form.

What happens when who you are, what you've been through, and what you bring to the table is more than enough? That connection becomes unbreakable. Your goals become their goals, and their goals become yours. That is the power of connection. Connect with those you are serving and, ultimately, those you are impacting. Create to connect, build to connect, and your impact on others will become unbreakable.

Take your seat, Continue on despite, Remain humble, Align your habits, Believe & Know your value, Create impact...

Direct your energy towards what's possible

It's easy to be swayed and distracted by the noise, the mess, what's going wrong, and what isn't going right. We can focus our energy on all those things and miss the lesson. When things aren't going the way we want them to, we must focus on what's important; the possibilities-our canvas. Even in the noise, the mess, you are still the author of your story, the painter. And as we know, you have the power to *continue on despite* it all.

And the lesson? The lesson is found in the 'how.' How were you able to continue on? How did you make it through? As you seek to create impact, make it a habit to direct your energy towards what's possible. Focus on what you can control. Find solutions, find alternate paths, when you are told no, continue on until you find someone who tells you yes.

Take your seat, Continue on despite, Remain humble, Align your habits, Believe & Know your value, Create impact...

Embrace criticism

Criticism is par for the course and is a well-known deterrent to those that have much to **give**, but choose not to act. It's not realistic to think that everyone will love who you have become, what you have to **give**, and how you will **give** it. So, you must embrace it. Embracing it does not mean you accept criticism as truth, but that you are open to evaluating its validity. Can you "take the good and leave the bad?" Do not let criticism stop you from creating impact. Remember your ability to exercise *humble confidence.*

As you create impact, be open to feedback and let it fuel your fire. The more your fire is fueled, the more impact you will create.

Take your seat, Continue on despite, Remain humble, Align your habits, Believe & Know your value, Create Impact...

Draw others with your "why?"

The reason behind your impact is equally as important as the impact you are creating. When days get tough, when challenge slaps you in the face, remembering the why behind it all gives you the strength to keep going. And as you create impact, people will be drawn to your why. They will find commonality in your journey, in why you have chosen to live the rest of your life creating at your canvas. The more you draw others, the more impact you will create.

Take your seat, Continue on despite, Remain humble, Align your habits, Believe & Know your value, Create impact...

Lift others "as you rise"

What good is it to achieve success, to stand at the top of a mountain, but find yourself all alone? Part of creating impact on others is found in the willingness to "lift as you rise." As you are given more responsibility, more influence, be willing to share your knowledge with others. They will become your greatest supporters, and long after you are gone, they will be equipped to continue your legacy.

As you create impact, rise…just don't rise alone.

Take your seat, Continue on despite, Remain humble, Align your habits, Believe & Know your value, Create impact...

Let the journey be the goal

Creating impact takes time and is a continuous journey in itself. There are no shortcuts, and you should not expect quick outcomes. Once you've made the decision to positively impact others, you are committing to doing what it takes for as long as it takes. And even when you have created an impact so palpable it can be felt by the masses, you must understand that you have simply reached another point in your journey, not the end. The goal is not to get to a point where you feel you've done enough. The goal is to continue to learn, continue to find ways through which you can create more impact.

Take your seat, Continue on despite, Remain humble, Align your habits, Believe & Know your value, Create impact...

A Great Responsibility

Creating impact comes with great responsibility. The more impact you create, the more influence you will hold. You must take this responsibility to heart. Your words and actions have the power to change the trajectories of others. If you abuse it, you could destroy those that look to you for guidance.

Remember your why, and if you ever believe you are out of alignment with it, seek counsel. It is an honor and a privilege to have the opportunity to impact others positively. Choose compassion, understanding, and "treat others the way you desire to be treated."

Take your seat, Continue on despite, Remain humble, Align your habits, Believe & Know your value, Create impact...

Now that we understand the components to creating impact, let's take a deeper look at the types of impact you can have on others.

First Impact

Your ability to impact others starts first with how you leave them. What impression do you leave behind? Harvard Psychologist Amy Cuddy suggests that first impressions are determined by whether a person feels they can trust you and if they find you likable. We, therefore, come back to authenticity. Leaving the best first impression of yourself requires your authenticity, and for you to be vulnerably **open**.

And yes, there was a period in my life where I was not **open**. I did not believe that I could be my authentic self. I was ashamed of my story, my pain, and my failures until I came to understand that my journey, what I had overcome, my mistakes, they taught me my greatest lessons and undoubtedly created my purpose.

And so wherever your start is...whatever mistakes you've made, you must know that we are all human and are all flawed. And despite our imperfections, we are designed and equipped to impact others. So I encourage you. Don't just leave the first impression, leave a lasting impression by being unapologetically you.

Take your seat, Continue on despite, Remain humble, Align your habits, Believe & Know your value, Create impact...

Working Impact

As a creator of impact, you will make many first impressions - first impacts. The question becomes, how will you continue to impact those you've met, whether directly or indirectly? The answer is in the availability and consistency of your work. Your working impact consists of providing others a platform to consume your content, message, and acumen, consistently. You can achieve this in many different ways. I share a few below:

- **Creating a web presence that clearly demonstrates your why and your what**

- **Creating a social media profile that clearly aligns with your why and your what**

- **Building a community**

- **Conducting community outreaches**

- **Organizing events**

- **Creating your products**

- **Offering services**

- **Offering mentorship**

Take your seat, Continue on despite, Remain humble, Align your habits, Believe & Know your value, Create impact...

Lasting Impact

Creating lasting impact lies in the quality of what you are **giving**. Here is where I say, follow your gut, listen to your inner voice, and ensure your content is an authentic representation of who you are and who you are becoming. Your work should be current and reflect your conviction. If you have viewpoints that have changed, share them unapologetically with your community.

What becomes evident, in this transparency, is that you demonstrate to those you are impacting, your growth and change. Your impact becomes palpable and not just a one-time event in their lives. Those you impact begin to grow with you. They evolve as you evolve. Your impact becomes continuous and, therefore, lasting.

Take your seat, Continue on despite, Remain humble, Align your habits, Believe & Know your value, Create impact...

What you have learned…

- *You have the power to create a life of greatness through impact.*

- *What to do when you are creating impact?*

  - *Dedicate your time to what gives your life, meaning and Purpose*

  - *Commit to growth; to become better*

  - *Establish connections through authenticity and alignment*

  - *Direct your energy towards what's possible.*

  - *Embrace criticism*

  - *Draw others with your "why?"*

  - *Lift others "as you rise"*

  - *Let the journey be the goal*

  - *Impact is a Great Responsibility*

- *Types of Impact*

  - *First Impact*

  - *Working Impact*

  - *Lasting Impact*

Take your seat, Continue on despite, Remain humble, Align your habits, Believe & Know your value, Create impact...

CHAPTER 7

THE GIVER'S SEAT

It's time...**Give this moment** a name...

Do you remember what my hope for you was at the very beginning? At the genesis of this journey? That by the time you finished being with me in this moment, you would know what? My friend, it has been my hope that as you read, you'd be inspired to discover and explore the deepest parts of who you are. To reach for your life's essence...the core that constitutes your meaning. To understand those things that create your value, the purpose of your existence, and what you will **give** to the world.

We've had an opportunity to dive into mindset. The power of the label. You have come to understand why you belong. That you can be humbly confident. That your habits and value matter. And that your greatness lives within the impact you will create, the legacy you'll leave behind.

And so, it is time...

It is time for you to pause...and ask yourself... What am I ready to **give**? What have I felt called to do, but have yet to explore? What is it that my life has **given** me; my abilities, gifts, knowledge, and skills? And from those, what is it that I want to **give** to the world?

And this time it is me that is with **you in your moment** as you take your seat...Go ahead... Take your seat as the **giver** you were born to be. The creak in the furniture, different; holding the weight of purpose and meaning for your life. You no longer seek validation from others. You only concern yourself with the core of your purpose... to create value from all that life has **given** you throughout your journey.

*Take your seat, Continue on despite, Remain humble, Align your habits, Believe & know your value, Create impact, **Give**...*

Pause *and ask yourself truly, unapologetically, no matter how grand, no matter how big, what is it that I am **ready** to **give**?*

That's it, tell me who you are...

MY LIFE...MY JOURNEY HAS **GIVEN** ME...

_____

_____

_____

_____

_____

_____

_____

_____

_____

_____

_____

_____

_____

_____

_____

_____

_____

_____

_____

_____

_____

_____

_____

_____

_____

_____

_____

_____

_____

AND FROM THAT, THIS IS WHAT I REALLY FEEL CALLED
TO DO...

_____

_____

_____

_____

_____

_____

_____

_____

_____

_____

_____

_____

_____

_____

_____

_____

_____

_____

_____

_____

_____

_____

_____

_____

_____

AND SO, THIS IS WHAT I'M READY TO **GIVE** TO THE WORLD...
IT DOESN'T MATTER THAT I DON'T HAVE EVERY DETAIL
MAPPED OUT.

I'M READY TO PAINT...

_____

_____

_____

_____

_____

_____

_____

_____

_____

_____

_____

_____

_____

_____

_____

_____

_____

_____

_____

_____

_____

_____

_____

_____

IT'S A START...I KNOW WHAT I WANT TO **GIVE** AND HERE'S MY WHY

_____

_____

_____

_____

_____

_____

_____

_____

_____

_____

_____

_____

_____

_____

_____

_____

_____

_____

_____

_____

_____

_____

_____

_____

_____

_____

_____

_____

That's it. It was this **pause**. It was at this same moment that I decided that the rest of my life would be lived from this seat. I was going to stay true to my newfound purpose. That whatever my future held, I could create it, and I could **give** it. That no matter what room I entered, no matter what table I had an opportunity to sit at, that I could create impact because the purpose of my life was to **give**. Never lose this moment; the feel of resolve in all its glory. Never lose what life has **given** you, what you feel called to **give,** and why you feel called to **give** it.

*Take your seat, Continue on despite, Remain humble, Align your habits, Believe & know your value, Create impact, **Give**…*

Before we move from this pause, allow me to share ways in which you can begin to **give** now and what you will unlock in your life by doing so.

Start with how you make others feel

A simple gesture of kindness with the sole intention of brightening up someone's day becomes a powerful demonstration that you are willing to **give** to others. To bring joy and happiness to humanity. *It's loving hard…beyond the surface; it's loving humanity.* Perhaps it's holding the door for the person behind you. Perhaps it's reaching out to colleagues and helping with a project that you aren't assigned to. Perhaps it's saying hello instead of simply walking by. Perhaps it's showing restraint instead of reacting. Perhaps it's letting annoying remarks go; they might just be having a bad day. Perhaps it's **giving** your time to someone who needs it. Perhaps it's taking time to volunteer in your community; serving and expecting nothing in return.

What you do matters…**give** kindness and develop your love for humanity. It is empathy. It is sympathy. It is going out of your way, without being obligated to...... to **feel** for the other and **do** for his/her gain.

*Take your seat, Continue on despite, Remain humble, Align your habits, Believe & know your value, Create impact, **Give**...*

Serve Others

Seek ways to serve others often. As you create, as you paint, begin to create for the betterment of humanity. Think big, and ask Yourself... "What can I create, build, that will touch more people?" And if fear sneaks in, whenyour creativity grows wide and deep, allow it to be your greatest compass.Let it lead you beyond what you envisioned. Allow it to free you from the bind of social convention as to what is possible. You must be fluid, willing to grow beyond, to transcend the present state of things, and create what is beyond. Painting on your canvas is a never-ending build towards greater. It is creating form that continually surpasses its previous state till the day you leave this earth. Because this act of **giving** brings clarity to your 'how'... how you make your mark on the world.

And you will begin to build and create your services, products, and all that you were born to **give**, and with those, you were meant to impact in mind.

*Take your seat, Continue on despite, Remain humble, Align your habits, Believe & know your value, Create impact, **Give**...*

Develop Appreciation

When you are **given** the opportunity to meet and connect with others, seek to find something in them. Something you can appreciate, about who they are, and how they have come to be there with you. Can you find something to appreciate in everyone? Yes... Yes, you can. It's understanding that we all have beginnings. We all have failures. We all have flaws, and we all have the opportunity to **give** what makes us great.

Take the time to ask questions and actively listen. Learn to hear what isn't spoken...hints to transcended information. Seek to understand why they may have certain beliefs, opinions, and perspectives. And then find joy in celebrating what you believe makes them great.

This is your ability to appreciate humanity...

Take your seat, Continue on despite, Remain humble, Align your habits, Believe & know your value, Create impact, **Give***...*

Unlock what you've always longed for

Go back to a moment in time where someone went above and beyond for you. It wasn't forced or asked for. The act was without provocation, it was unexpected, but was somehow right on time. What did you feel? Yes, that right there. What did it feel like?

Now, imagine being on the other end of that exchange, the **giver**. The creator of positive spontaneity. Responsible for being the source of what we as humans long for daily, the person that is responsible for affecting happiness in others. How would you feel when you're bold enough to **give** without expecting anything in return?

When you live your life, creating with others in mind...A life committed to **giving** so that others may feel joy; so that they may experience happiness. What would you feel? To know that you are responsible for sparking someone else's flame...You unlock happiness and fulfillment in your own life. Every time you **give**, every time you brighten up someone's day. Every time you seize an opportunity to serve unconditionally... Every time you seize the opportunity to appreciate humanity, the happiness you cause is amplified and reflected back into your own life. Something you simply cannot gain from your possessions. You see, the purpose of your life has never been in what you could gain, but in what you could find delight in **giving**.

*Take your seat, Continue on despite, Remain humble, Align your habits, Believe & Know your value, Create Impact, **Give**...*

CHAPTER 8

AGAIN AND AGAIN

Down in the valley… Up through the climb…In the steps that you take towards the unknown…All the work you will do at your canvas… In all the risk… In all the "blood, sweat, and tears," you'll experience along the way… Every time you fall down you must be willing to do it, over and over again. To get back up, dust yourself off, and keep going. And even when you are at what others will consider your peak, you must decide that the journey is worth continuing. You find new mountains to climb… because you know you cannot attain perfection… the journey towards **giving** all that you can give… the pursuit; that's the essence of your life.

You see, it is not a question of if, it is only a question of when. When things get tough…When you are faced with unexpected challenges and storms…When others seem to have let you down…When you let yourself down… Do you have what it takes, right then and there, to get back up and keep going instead of **giving** up? Are you built with the resilience to carry on and ever stroke at your canvas?

YES - Remember what your life has given you. Remember what is by your side; all your cans of paint - your tools. There is no better person more equipped than you on your journey to get back up and do it again. And by continuing, you begin to adapt and spot the patterns; you learn… equipping yourself with what it takes for the next mountain… not if it comes, but when it comes.

This is a commitment that you are willing to remember what you are made of. That your greatness is not defined in your fall, but your willingness to get back up and run towards your purpose.

It's not that I've never failed, I've failed. It's that if I live my life not will-ing to fail, I'll never **give** *myself the opportunity to grow from getting back up.*

What will you do with what you have?

"I've missed more than 9000 shots in my career. I've lost almost 300 games. 26 times, I've been trusted to take the game-winning shot and missed. I've failed over and over and over again in my life. And that is why I succeed." - Michael Jordan

"Our greatest glory is not in never falling, but in rising, every time we fall." - Confucious

"I don't believe in failure. It is not failure if you enjoyed the process." - Oprah Winfrey

In this chapter, we will look at two important areas that are under your complete control. In the fall and throughout your journey, exercising your power in these areas will help you get back up.

Exercise The Power of Positivity

It's easy to beat yourself up when you've fallen down. Yes, we can, at times, be our own worst enemy because of how we see our challenge and what we believe we are capable of in that particular storm. To lose your attitude when things get tough. To focus on weakness instead of strength. To believe that this fall will be the one that keeps you down. Those negative beliefs will not serve you in hard times and will prevent you from finding the lesson in the fall… appreciating the growth from the lesson…and getting back up to go at it again.

If you find yourself in what seems like a dark moment, exercise the power of your positivity. Believe that this moment in time has a purpose in your life. Believe that there is a lesson to be learned. Believe that you will be better after you've made it through. Remember, the "how you overcame" becomes the lesson, the tool you can use in the future. This positive thinking will help you maintain your attitude and help you direct your focus towards what's really important - getting back up, my friend.

And once you've exercised your power to be positive even in the face of challenge, it is even more critical that you surround yourself with others that will also pour positivity into your life, into your journey. Important in the fall, but equally important throughout the journey. When others dish out negative energy, these are the steps you can take towards exercising your positivity.

- *Set and enforce boundaries.*

One of the greatest lessons I've learned on my journey came from an interview Oprah Winfrey **gave** years ago. Where she spoke about her responsibility to herself and how she allowed others to make her feel.

We all have this responsibility. If someone makes you feel negative. If they take your joy. If they kick you when you are down. If they are only around when things are going well but choose not to support you, hear you, and understand you in the difficult times…You must set boundaries to protect yourself. What does this mean?

It means that you have the right to let others know how they are making you feel. And if they are unable to support you in both the good and bad times, then it is your responsibility to determine if their presence at this point in your journey is required. You own how you allow others to impact you. You control the energies that are channeled towards you and their continued presence in your life. No one else owns that responsibility. To expose yourself to hurt and negativity is a statement in of itself; that you believe you deserve the mess, the lack of support, and emotional instability.

You deserve to have positive people in your life who support you on your journey. You deserve unwavering, unconditional love. Meaningful connections that support you in pursuit of your passions. And so, you must set that boundary and enforce it in the fall and throughout your journey.

*Take your seat, Continue on despite, Remain humble, Align your habits, Believe & know your value, Create impact, **Give**, Get up…*

- ***Respond mindfully – don't just react.***

We spoke briefly about restraint earlier on, but restraint really is a powerful tool for protecting your emotions and your energy. When others attempt to throw negative energy your way, and you do not respond, it throws them off. They aren't getting the response from you that they were hoping for. It becomes a demonstration of your strength and character, but equally a lesson to you both, that negativity is powerless in the face of greatness.

Instead of reacting with emotion, exercise your ability to pause and respond mindfully. Meaning, take the time to ask yourself, what lesson can be learned? Is this an opportunity for me to demonstrate my character and my strength? And if a response is required...what response would deliver the best outcome? This pause will ensure that you have taken the time to think and learn from the experience.

In the fall, it's easy to react, but that won't serve your purpose. You are powerful, my friend. Live in your power. Live in your strength.

*Take your seat, Continue on despite, Remain humble, Align your habits, Believe & know your value, Create impact, **Give**, Get up...*

- *Give Positivity*

There will be times when others are simply unaware of where you are on your journey, and their interaction with you may trigger negative feelings in you, unintentionally. In that case, you must exercise your ability to **give** positivity even in that moment. Yes, it is asking you to **give** of yourself by bringing positivity even when you don't feel like doing so. A change in topic. Asking how you can serve that individual or brighten up their day. Remembering a great moment and reminiscing together.

In the fall and throughout the journey, there may be times where you will have to **give** positivity to the situation. Some call this, "being the bigger person," I call this choosing to exercise your power always.

*Take your seat, Continue on despite, Remain humble, Align your habits, Believe & know your value, Create impact, **Give**, Get up...*

- ***Focus on solutions, recognize distractions.***

Negativity comes in many forms. What you've heard me refer to as the noise and the mess. More than trying to hurt you, the noise and mess can be meant to distract you. To get you off course, to urge you to **give** in to the tendency to stay down when you've fallen and to redirect your focus towards things that have no meaning…that carry no weight.

You must learn to recognize distractions early and often. Those that are uncomfortable with you knowing who you are and the pursuit of who you are becoming.

In the fall and throughout the journey, you've got to focus on the solutions. Don't let distractions take you off course.

*Take your seat, Continue on despite, Remain humble, Align your habits, Believe & know your value, Create impact, **Give**, Get up...*

- ***Remember whose labels and opinions matter***

Your ability to remain positive in these moments of your journey requires mental fortitude. The strength you derive from certainty in who you are and where you know you are going. Irrespective of the negative labels that may be thrown your way, you must remember whose labels and opinions matter. Your sense of self and happiness cannot be derived from the opinions of others. Instead, stand in your strength and your identity.

In the fall and throughout the journey, always remember **your** beliefs are the only beliefs that matter.

*Take your seat, Continue on despite, Remain humble, Align your habits, Believe & know your value, Create impact, **Give**, Get up...*

- ***Focus on impacting others not changing them***

For those in your life that you are hoping to change, you've got to know that changing someone isn't your job. It is your impact that has the power to effect change in others. But effecting change does not equate to you doing the work for them...If you do the work for them, they are unable to truly appreciate what it takes to change. Things that are beyond your control are beyond your control.

In the fall and throughout your journey, you must focus on what you cancontrol, your impact on others.

*Take your seat, Continue on despite, Remain humble, Align your habits, Believe & know your value, Create impact, **Give**, Get up...*

Do The Work

- ***In the fall, remind yourself of what you are looking to give to others and why***

   Think about those that will be touched by you and allow that to keep your fire going. Let it motivate you to get up again and do the work. Understand that the legacy you are looking to leave behind is directly dependent upon your ability to keep going.

*Take your seat, Continue on despite, Remain humble, Align your habits, Believe & know your value, Create impact, **Give**, Get up...*

- ***Be honest with yourself***

When you've fallen down, you must acknowledge where you are. If you need help or guidance, you must be willing to be honest with yourself and seek out the help you need.

*Take your seat, Continue on despite, Remain humble, Align your habits, Believe & know your value, Create impact, **Give**, Get up...*

- *Stay Open*

We know the importance of being **open** versus boxed. As you work to get back up again, you can expect to grow in the process. Be **open** in the climb back up. The climb may require you to do things differently...you will evolve in your thinking, allow yourself to see things differently. Your willingness to be flexible removes delay and gets you to your next level of growth, much quicker.

*Take your seat, Continue on despite, Remain humble, Align your habits, Believe & know your value, Create impact, **Give**, Get up...*

- *Stay Disciplined*

Discipline, we know, is established through our habits. If you fall, you may need to establish new habits that align with your purpose. Or you may need to exercise existing habits that will help you get back up.

*Take your seat, Continue on despite, Remain humble, Align your habits, Believe & know your value, Create impact, **Give**, Get up...*

Things to remember...

No matter how many times you fall, it is you who controls how you behave when you are down, and when you are getting back up.

Leverage these tips to ensure you get back up again and again and stay positive along the way.

*Take your seat, Continue on despite, Remain humble, Align your habits, Believe & know your value, Create impact, **Give**, Get up...*

CHAPTER 9

ALIGN AND UNLEASH

You've learned the power of positivity and how to apply it to your life when others are not aligned with you. Here, we will dive into the importance of aligning with others to maximize your impact, positioning yourself to unleash all that is within you, through collaboration.

What does it mean to align? And who should you align with?

Alignment shows that your willingness to *appreciate humanity* has afforded you a very special ability. It is the ability to recognize your skills or the lack of them while being completely **open** to acknowledging others' strengths, what makes them great, and finding ways to collaborate... Expanding your impact and theirs.

Think about that, collaborating to the point that *your goals become their goals, and their goals become yours*. Imagine the impact that you will have on others, but most importantly, on each other through this alignment. The "lift as you rise." And if you are going to "lift as you rise," you will need to know who to lift along your journey. We will look at this in more detail, but let's first dive into alignment through collaboration.

Collaboration

Collaboration, in its simplest form, occurs when two or more individuals willingly come together and contribute their strengths, acumen, and perspectives, collectively, its value, for the benefit of a shared objective & goal.

So, what does this look like?

Perhaps it's working with a colleague on creatives for a marketing campaign. The goal is to tell a story to your consumer base that accurately reflects the value your organization brings to its consumers. Say, your strength is in the development of the graphics, your colleague's in the development of the content. Together, you work hand in hand, aligned, not seeing the other's strength as intrusive or intimidating, but as why you are better together. And the more you create together, the more your consumers begin to respond. Your organization accredits the success of your campaign to your collaboration, and your impact together becomes undeniable.

What I've just described is the value and importance of alignment as you seek to widen your impact. What does that mean? It means that you can't do "it" alone. No one can do "it" alone. And so, trust becomes an important component to scaling your impact. I once wrote a piece on scaling through trust. And what I shared was that as an entrepreneur, I had to learn that, yes, I was **given** the vision. But if I wanted to grow that vision, whether a company, community initiative, or work project, I was going to need people who could bring their greatness to the table. And where I was weak, they could be strong. I had to be willing to align, to be **open** and transparent about needing help in order to create the impact I was looking to create. To lower my ego and embrace what made others great.

That transparency did three things. It **gave** others the space to choose if they wanted to align with me. I came to the table, **giving** them the trust they deserved because of the choice they made to align. And it allowed others to understand the value they would bring to the impact we were now looking to create together.

That type of alignment and collaboration amplifies the fire in you both. And when you have not just one, but two, three, hundreds, thousands, millions of people all on fire...you have unleashed impact so powerful that it moves the masses. And when you create an impact that touches the masses, you would have started the process of leaving your mark.

Once you've identified the impact you are looking to create, trust those who are aligned with that vision. Through that alignment, scale your impact by being **open,** completely willing to embrace the strengths in others, providing them a platform to bring the very best of who they are to the table.

*Take your seat, Continue on despite, Remain humble, Align your habits, Believe & know your value, Create impact, **Give**, Get up, Make your mark...*

Let's look closer at why alignment-collaboration-works and why your impact scales.

The Benefits of Collaborating

Collaboration helps us problem-solve

Have you ever run into a problem and had no one to turn to? Perhaps you've made progress on a project you are working on, but you encounter what you perceive as a roadblock. You see no path forward and are unable to find a workable solution. What do you do?

Collaboration affords us the opportunity to find solutions. The best thing we can do is ask for help. And in asking for help, we gain different perspectives. Those perspectives **give** us the insight we need to find those solutions together. What we perceived as roadblocks become solvable. In the process, you've grown through collaboration and can *continue on despite*.

It's never the mountain that stops you. It is simply that you stopped. Keep going. Your greatest lessons come from the climb.

*Take your seat, Continue on despite, Remain humble, Align your habits, Believe & know your value, Create impact, **Give**, Get up, Make your mark...*

Collaboration brings us closer together

What an incredible bond that can be formed between those who are willing to come together and collaborate. To reach a goal together. To walk a journey together no matter how rough the terrain. To solve what appears to be unsolvable, together. And when you do find a solution, imagine the connection that is made and trust that is established.

When you collaborate with others, the process itself brings you closer together. It is the appreciation you have for the work you have both put in. In the process, there is growth, but most importantly, connection.

*Take your seat, Continue on despite, Remain humble, Align your habits, Believe & know your value, Create impact, **Give**, Get up, Make your mark...*

Collaboration increases our acumen

Learn from other's experiences. Experiences that are filled with different insights and developed acumen. Collaborating with others **gives** us the opportunity to learn new things because those lessons are being shared freely to drive desired outcomes.

When you are given the opportunity to collaborate, come ready to learn.Don't miss this opportunity. Even if it's a lunch meeting or simply connecting over a cup of coffee. Come ready to take notes, and approach the connection as a student. The more you learn, the more impact that can be created by the collective.

*Take your seat, Continue on despite, Remain humble, Align your habits, Believe & know your value, Create impact, **Give**, Get up, Make your mark...*

Collaboration creates new opportunities

When you are **open** to collaborating with others, you naturally create new opportunities for yourself. Some are perhaps immediate, while others are developed over time. It's doing the work together today, and as a result, creating new or additional paths forward over the long term...immediate impact and impact you are yet to discover and create.

There have been those I have met, collaborated with, and created a connection with. And because of that connection, opportunities that I did not expect **opened** up for me.

*Take your seat, Continue on despite, Remain humble, Align your habits, Believe & know your value, Create impact, **Give**, Get up, Make your mark...*

Collaboration makes us more efficient

I look at efficiency as operating in such a way that everything you do is done with meaning and purpose. Your actions have intent behind them and are aligned with the end goal, the impact you are looking to create...And because those actions are in complete alignment with your impact, your results are powerful, timely, and effective. Meaning, the outcomes you desired come to fruition right on time in the most optimal way.

As we come to see the benefits of collaboration, it becomes clear that working with others for a common goal not only maximizes individual efforts but also minimizes the time in which those efforts are realized. Dividing up the work that is required, finding solutions faster, and even expanding upon the vision.

*Take your seat, Continue on despite, Remain humble, Align your habits, Believe & know your value, Create impact, **Give**, Get up, Make your mark...*

Now the Who...

I'd like to take us back to the draw. Who we will draw as we approach the world completely on fire. While we are doing the work, painting at our canvas, and **giving** through impact, who will draw close because of our fire? We know that there are those who will be touched by what we do and those who may smear us with negativity and opposition.

I'd like to look at these two crowds again and **give** you some perspective as to why there is benefit from working with both.

The "You inspire me" Crowd

This community of individuals will look to you first for inspiration. They would have seen or heard of the impact you are creating, and they will want to be a part of it. They will naturally be drawn to you and feel connected with you because of your message, your journey, and how you **give**. Simply put, you resonate with them in some capacity.

As a result, they support your work and the cause. The "why" behind what you are **giving**. They are aligned with you, and the more you unleash what you were destined to **give**, the more they are willing to help. It is without question that you align yourself with this community and find ways in which you can create more impact in their lives by lifting those who become so inspired by what you do, that they seek to do the same for others. Those that come to you wanting mentorship and coaching, so that they too, can create impact; those are the individuals you should lift along with you.

Take your seat, Continue on despite, Remain humble, Align your habits, Believe & know your value, Create impact, **Give,** *Get up, Make your mark...*

But what about those who secretly want to see you fail or are uncomfortable with you knowing who you are? Is there any benefit in collaborating with this crowd?

The *"You make me uncomfortable" Crowd*

This community of individuals will meet you with opposition... opposition that may be very direct or perhaps, be presented as support but hides their desire to see you fail. Is there any benefit with collaborating with direct or indirect opposition? Yes, I believe there is, and here's why.

Let's first look at direct opposition from the vantage point of...direct opposition does not mean you should **give** up, but should be seen as an opportunity; a platform to both grow and demonstrate your growth at the same time. Direct opposition may come in many forms. The questions becomes, how will you respond? Will you allow that individual to distract you from what's important, or will you see the opposition as an opportunity to demonstrate your resolve? In this case, the collaboration is not in working together for a common goal but describes aligning yourself with the opportunity to grow... the lessons that can be learned from this challenge. Not engaging in the negativity by matching the negativity, but meeting it with resolve, grace, and respect. This not only strengthens you and teaches you how to interact with someone who may want to see you fail, but also teaches that individual that negativity is only powerful if the other person allows it to be. This becomes a powerful lesson for you both.

And in my own journey, I have had the opportunity to interact with this crowd, and I can only show my gratitude to those that showed opposition, because I became stronger from it. And because I was not moved and stood firm in my resolve, some of those individuals came back to wish me well. Why? Because anyone can be unexpectedly inspired, especially by someone fully committed to creating positive impact in the face of challenge.

Let's look at indirect opposition...This opposition can be a challenge in itself to spot. However, my rule of thumb is to always trust your intuition. A Red flag, is a red flag. I have found the need to lead with empathy with this type of opposition. Why? Because not everyone will initially understand your fire… Not everyone will be comfortable being around someone with strong conviction. And so, I've learned to not take this type of opposition personally. Instead, I find fulfillment in leading with empathy and extending my hand-aligning through the demonstration of kindness and never-ending willingness to share my "why."

Whether you are faced with genuine support from others or find yourself drawing opposition, consider how you can grow from all of the connections you make. See challenge as an opportunity to become better. Seek to empathize when you are unsure of what you are being faced with.

And know that as long as you don't **give** credence to negativity, even in the face of opposition, you can remain poised in your greatness. Our impact is stronger **together**.

What you have learned…

- *Alignment sets the foundation for collaboration*

- *The more you collaborate, the more your impact is maximized, and the more you can unleash all that is inside of you*

- *The benefits of collaboration*

  - *Helps us Problem-Solve*

  - *Brings us closer together*

- *Increases our acumen*

- *Creates new opportunity*

- *Makes us more efficient*

• *You can find ways to align with both crowds*

  - *You Inspire Me Crowd*

  - *You Make Me Uncomfortable Crowd*

*Take your seat, Continue on despite, Remain humble, Align your habits, Believe & know your value, Create impact, **Give**, Get up, Make your mark...*

CHAPTER 10

COLLISION

COLLISION: Two forces colliding head-on...

Creation cannot exist without two or more things coming together. This is not an assertion of religion or a declaration of how the earth came to be. We all have our own beliefs. But what is true, what is irrefutable, what is universal, is that **nothing can be created without two or more things coming together**.

Here is my belief...

In order to create anything, there must be some type of collision. Your very existence, a powerful example of what can come from this type of force. What did it take to create you? The egg of your mother and the sperm of your father. Collision. Water, the presence of Hydrogen and Oxygen. Collision. And for the purposes of our meeting, your journey, you colliding with the path that you have taken. Collision.

Irrespective of how those two things lived void of each other...Once they collide, something new is created. And for the rest of your life, you've got to know that the power to create what's ahead of you is already living on the inside of you. It is in your genetic makeup-the reflection of creation in its purest form. If you have ever told your-self, "Maybe I'm not cut out for greatness. Maybe I'm not enough. Maybe I was not born to be great at anything." I must ask you..." How could that be true when you, yourself, are a direct result of an intentional collision-containing the very power that created you?

Now, you may be asking...Why did you choose the word, collision? I chose collision because its impact is hard and head-on...Its after-math? Well, it creates whatever will be with intent...There is no hesi-tation. There is no turning back. The result of a collision will always produce something of purpose and meaning because what comes after is never by accident.

You, too, have a door. It's yours, no one else's. It will never be opened by anyone but you. This is your purpose. Take your leap. Run towards the unknown. How will you know it's yours? You'll see its light, You will feel it's call. And you'll know, before knowing what everything will look like on the other side, before you know who will be waiting in support of it, that it's yours. Live your purpose and gain the fulfillment you have been seeking. There is no better time than right now.

Now in your control...
I knew that the world wasn't going to just happen to me, but I was going to happen to the world.

I want you to know that you have the power to collide. To happen to the world. And the very power that created you, affords you that same power to create what only you can imagine-impact. How do you create impact? The guide you have been **given**, those my friend, ways in which you can leverage the power that is within you to run... To never look back...To run hard and head-on towards your purpose. To collide.

*Take your seat, Continue on despite, Remain humble, Align your habits, Believe & know your value, Create impact, **Give**, Get up, Make your mark, Collide...*

Before we move into our final moments together, let's pause and look closely at what is now in your control.

What you learn

From this day forward, you are in complete control of what you know and understand, at any point in time. Remember, you will never reach a point where there is nothing more to learn. Go out and collide with knowledge. Pushing yourself outside what is comfortable and familiar. You don't need anyone's permission to gain new understanding. One of the best inventions out there is the internet. I consider it the great equalizer. If you want to learn how to create impact in finance, Google it. If you want to learn how to create impact in conservation, Google it. If you want to learn how to create impact by starting a business in any vertical, Google it. Seek it out, and you will find answers. Be willing to fall down and learn from getting back up. There is nothing you cannot learn when you put your mind to it. All you have to do is **give** it your all. Sit at your canvas and create.

*Take your seat, Continue on despite, Remain humble, Align your habits, Believe & know your value, Create impact, **Give**, Get up, Make your mark, Collide…*

Your work

From this day forward, you are in complete control of the work you put in. No matter where you are on your journey right now, it is you who controls what you do. If what you feel called to do makes you afraid, allow that fear to be your greatest compass. And if what you feel called to do makes others afraid, allow their fear to also be your greatest compass. No one can stop you from running towards your purpose, except you. In the face of opposition, stand in your power, in your positivity and *continue on despite*. Collide with the work, the steps it will take to fulfill your purpose.

*Take your seat, Continue on despite, Remain humble, Align your habits, Believe & know your value, Create impact, **Give**, Get up, Make your mark, Collide…*

Your Fortitude

From this day forward, you are in complete control of getting back up. When you fall down, there is not a single person on this planet that can keep you down. Let your previous falls be your sources of strength. Remember who you are always and collide with the tools your life has afforded you. Redefine failure. And when you see trouble coming, you are still in control. *Run through your mountain.*

*Take your seat, Continue on despite, Remain humble, Align your habits, Believe & Know your value, Create Impact, **Give**, Get up, Make your mark, Collide…*

Your Time

From this day forward, you are in complete control of your time. No one owns you, and therefore, no one owns your time. Be responsible and exercise discipline. Do what is required of you, your work, but set boundaries. Outside of your work, your time is your time. Form habits that allow you to create. Collide with every day you are **given**. And see your twenty-four hours as an opportunity. An opportunity to create what you will **give** to the world. .

Take your seat, Continue on despite, Remain humble, Align your habits, Believe & know your value, Create impact, **Give***, Get up, Make your mark, Collide...*

Your Exploration

From this day forward, you are in complete control of your exploration. Explore what inspires you unexpectedly. Another call towards your greatness. Let no one take your curiosity.

Collide with your intuition. In other words, trust yourself the first time and every time. Understand that if it were not meant to come from you, you wouldn't dream it. You wouldn't envision it. You wouldn't feel it.

Take your seat, Continue on despite, Remain humble, Align your habits, Believe & know your value, Create impact, **Give***, Get up, Make your mark, Collide...*

Your Energy

From this day forward, you are in complete control of your energy and whether you welcome their positivity or their negativity. You do not need anyone's permission to protect your energy. One of the most sacred parts of you are the emotions that you bring to any connection. Those are in your control. Collide with yourself. Do not allow anyone to move you from who you are and desire to be at any **given** moment.

*Take your seat, Continue on despite, Remain humble, Align your habits, Believe & know your value, Create impact, **Give**, Get up, Make your mark, Collide…*

Your Response

From this day forward, you are in complete control of how you respond to any situation. In the face of negativity, whether directly or indirectly, it is you who is in control of your response. Remember the power of your restraint. And if you do respond, remember the power of your alignment. Collide with your power and **give** positivity even in the face of negativity.

*Take your seat, Continue on despite, Remain humble, Align your habits, Believe & know your value, Create impact, **Give**, Get up, Make your mark, Collide…*

Your love

From this day forward, you are in complete control of your love. Love yourself first, so that you will know how to love others. Set boundaries and standards. Love others close or, if needed, from afar. Love your work, because when you love anything, you will do what it takes to **give** all that you were born to **give** to it. Collide with love and let it create the place from which it comes.

*Take your seat, Continue on despite, Remain humble, Align your habits, Believe & know your value, Create impact, **Give**, Get up, Make your mark, Collide...*

Your appreciation

From this day forward, you are in complete control of how you appreciate all things. Your life... All that it has **given** you...The good times, but most importantly, the bad times...The falls...The bumps in the road...The mountains...The storms...Others...Humanity...What makes them great...the opportunity to align...The impact that you will create. Collide with empathy. Never put yourself above anyone, and when you rise, lift at the same time.

*Take your seat, Continue on despite, Remain humble, Align your habits, Believe & know your value, Create impact, **Give**, Get up, Make your mark, Collide...*

Your Decisions

From this day forward, you are in complete control of every decision you make. Never let anyone decide for you...Who you will be...What you **give**...Where you will **give**...When you will **give** it. Collide with intention. Anticipate the outcome of your actions and choose to create positivity instead of negativity. .

*Take your seat, Continue on despite, Remain humble, Align your habits, Believe & know your value, Create impact, **Give**, Get up, Make your mark, Collide...*

Your voice

From this day forward, you are in complete control of your voice. Your message...The story that you will tell. No one can quiet your voice. Speak...Collide with your conviction...Know that your words are powerful. They form your beliefs. Use your voice wisely. Do not tear others down. When you speak, speak from your heart. Let your words have meaning. And when you are **given** the opportunity to tell your story, let your authenticity guide you through it.

Take your seat, Continue on despite, Remain humble, Align your habits, Believe & know your value, Create impact, **Give***, Get up, Make your mark, Collide...*

Your Fire

From this day forward, you are in complete control of your fire. The flame that **gives** you presence...What inspires those you are privileged to meet. Let no one dampen your flame. Your life, your existence, is all the validation you need to keep going. Your experiences, all of them; let those things set you on fire...And let them keep you on fire. Collide with the purpose of your life. Your purpose will always be bigger than any mountain.

Take your seat, Continue on despite, Remain humble, Align your habits, Believe & know your value, Create impact, **Give***, Get up, Make your mark, Collide...*

Your Openness

From this day forward, you are in complete control to live the rest of your life, **open**. **Open** to all the possibilities that exist before and ahead of you. You will reach many mountain tops with this mindset. Be willing to grow...To add to...To make changes...To develop new habits...To be flexible...Collide with your growth & development. No one will ever be able to box you in if you decide to live life completely **open**.

*Take your seat, Continue on despite, Remain humble, Align your habits, Believe & know your value, Create impact, **Give**, Get up, Make your mark, Collide...*

Your resolve

From this day forward, you are in complete control of your resolve. As you live the rest of your life creating, your belief system will lead you to new heights. Never let another's lack of understanding break your resolve. Collide with your beliefs. Hold yourself accountable. Check your beliefs always. Be comfortable with asking yourself, "What do I believe now?"

*Take your seat, Continue on despite, Remain humble, Align your habits, Believe & know your value, Create impact, **Give**, Get up, Make your mark, Collide...*

Your habits

From this day forward, you are in complete control of the habits you make room for in your life. You and you alone are responsible for what you do. Make room for those habits that serve your purpose. Acknowledge the ones that do not, but your focus must be on creating habits that align with where you are going. Collide with accountability and create discipline in your life.

*Take your seat, Continue on despite, Remain humble, Align your habits, Believe & know your value, Create impact, **Give**, Get up, Make your mark, Collide...*

Your Canvas

From this day forward, you are in complete control of the rest of your life. Your life is your canvas. If you **give** to it, it will **give** to you...Paint...Paint often. Do not let others take you off course. Amid the noise, the mess, create. Collide with your moment. This is your moment...Even if your canvas is without color, you control what's next. Pick up your brush and make your life a masterpiece. Leave your legacy...Make sure you are never forgotten and always felt.

Take your seat, Continue on despite, Remain humble, Align your habits, Believe & know your value, Create impact, **Give**, *Get up, Make your mark, Collide...*

How do you feel?

I know the feeling...To realize your purpose...What you want to **give**...And now to know that you really do have what it takes. All of these things...All that you have control over, have just raised your stakes. They are those cans of paint that once lay by your side with the tops on. Use them...Bring them with you always. In everything you do...Bring all of you to the table - those components that truly make you great.

Take your seat, Continue on despite, Remain humble, Align your habits, Believe & know your value, Create impact, **Give**, *Get up, Make your mark, Collide...*

What you have learned...

COLLISION: *Two forces colliding head-on...*
Collide
- *Now in your control...*

    ◦ *What you learn*

    ◦ *Your work*

- *Your fortitude*

- *Your time*

- *Your exploration*

- *Your energy*

- *Your response*

- *Your love*

- *Your appreciation*

- *Your decisions*

- *Your voice*

- *Your fire*

- *Your openness*

- *Your resolve*

- *Your habits*

- *Your canvas*

*Take your seat, Continue on despite, Remain humble, Align your habits, Believe & know your value, Create impact, **Give**, Get up, Make your mark, Collide...*

CHAPTER 11

THE TABLE

MY LETTER TO YOU

Dearest Reader,

In just a moment, you'll be **given** your final moment of pause. One of self-reflection. This time, to share what you have gained from our time together. And once you've shared it here, I'll ask you to take it a step further and share it with the world. As a final declaration, that for the rest of your life, you'll never truly believe that you can't accomplish whatever you put your mind, heart, and soul into. That in all doubt, your own unique experiences-your life- will continue to set you on fire. You will live life from the **Giver's Seat**. You will paint. You will create the impact you were born to create. Fear will be your greatest compass. And your journey, all that you will **give from this day forward**, will leave the world a better place.

Before your final pause…

Thank you for **Meet**ing **Me At The Table**. The beginning of our connection, the *first impact*. Here, the sharing of ideas, perspectives, passions, beliefs, and purpose with you has been one of the greatest moments of my life. For this opportunity, I am thankful. I am humbled. Humbled that our lives…Everything we have experienced along our paths has brought us together. Irrespective of our individual stories, here we are.

You see, **The Table**, right from the very beginning of our meeting, has represented the place where **connections** are made, the point of collision.

> *Connections are powerful and go beyond "relationships."*
> *To be connectedwith another human being means that*
> *a safe space has beencreated to share ideas, opinions,*
> *passions, needs, weaknesses, and Strengths. And within*
> *that connection, there is a genuine appreciation for what*
> *makes that person* **great***, who they are now, and who*
> *they seek to become in the future. It is authenticity and*
> *expression of humanity in its purest form.*

CONNECTION… It is where anything can be painted… Where anything can be created. When you set out to create your own impact, after you have decided how you will live the rest of your life, you must first **connect** with yourself, understanding what it is you believe.

So many people struggle with identifying who they are and where they should begin. From this day forward, that never has to be your reality. You will always be the answer. Because **you are** the GREATNESS in this story. It is your **greatness** that has collided with the impact I desired to create in this moment.

Do You See It **Now?**

Collision... Where two or more things collide. *Unplanned but timely, unexpected, but destined...***without hesitation**. And so the question(s) becomes...What have we created from this moment? In this **connection**? From this collision?

Beyond this point, you will take your final pause, but you should know my final belief...I believe that no matter where you are on your journey right now, you will always know you have the power to create what this **connection** has started...That what will be has already begun. Deep down, you will always know that GREATNESS lives within you, and as long as you are willing to collide with your purpose, without hesitation, you will leave a mark so great it can't be forgotten.

Collide,

Christine Sanni,
Founder of #greatlymade

#GREATLYMADE MANTRA

WE ACKNOWLEDGE THAT WE ARE NOT BORN GREAT BUT BORN WITH THE COMPONENTS TO BECOME GREAT. THAT WE ARE NOT DEFINED BY INDIVIDUAL EXPERIENCES IN OUR LIVES, BUT BY A COMBINATION OF THE TOOLS WE GAIN FROM EACH OF THOSE EXPERIENCES, BEING GREATLY MADE IN UNDERSTANDING THAT GREATNESS IS DEVELOPED OVER TIME. IT IS ACCOUNTABILITY, DISCIPLINE, THE ABILITY TO SERVE OTHERS, AND MAKE AN IMPACT. BEING GREATLY MADE IS DOING THE WORK, CALLING UPON ALL THESE THINGS, AND NEVER TURNING THEM OFF.

YOUR FINAL PAUSE

THIS CONNECTION HAS **GIVEN** ME...

I AM THANKFUL FOR...

_____
_____
_____
_____
_____
_____
_____
_____
_____
_____
_____
_____
_____
_____
_____
_____
_____
_____
_____
_____
_____
_____.

*Take your seat, Continue on despite, Remain humble, Align your habits, Believe & Know your value, Create Impact, **Give**, Get up, Make your mark, Collide, Connect...*

CHOOSE

Trials are not designed to determine our worth, but to demonstrate our transformative strength. This is your call. This is your moment to find your greatness and never turn it off. To not live life, but create a life that inspires the masses.

I understand that every person that meets me here will have their own unique story. What brought them to *the table*. A journey filled with its own sources of pain, failures, successes, and beliefs. Even now, your beliefs may be holding you back with doubts and fears that are preventing you from seeing your greatness. How do you move forward? Right here, right now, at this moment?

My friend...You must simply **choose**. Just as I had to choose, that for the rest of my life, I would **give** instead of take. In an era where your product nor your possessions, will be seen as your highest currency and greatest asset, you must **choose** that the value you will bring is in the power of your ability to connect with humanity. **Choose** connection, at home, at work, in your community, in your relation-ships, and in all that you do. Live life from the **Giver's** seat and con-nection won't be a one-time thing, but a habit.

THIS IS YOUR CALL TO GREATNESS

Take your seat, Continue on despite, Remain humble, Align your habits, Believe & Know your value, Create Impact, **Give**, *Get up, Make your mark, Collide, Connect, & Choose.*

Before we go... Your final declaration.

*Take a moment to tell the world how you intend to live the rest of your life. Tell them what you will **give**. Post your declaration on your favorite social media platform with **#greatlymade**. I look forward to reading your post.*

WORKING IMPACT

LET'S STAY CONNECTED

If you are not part of our growing community, please join us via Facebook by searching #GREATLYMADE and request to become a member. I interact with this community daily and we would be happy for you to join us.

Social Media: (Follow, Like, Share)
Facebook @therealchristinesanni
Instagram @therealchristinesanni
Twitter @therealcsanni
YouTube Channel: (Like and Subscribe) Christine Sanni

PR & Media

Email: book@christinesanni.com

Speaking Engagement

Email: book@christinesanni.com
Website: www.christinesanni.com

Products

Greatness Learned.

E-Learning Platform

Business Center

Tools to help you take your business to the next level.

Private Coaching

www.christinesanni.com

Live Free Group Coaching

Streamed Live: Twitter, Instagram, YouTube

Saturdays @11:00 AM EST

REFERENCES

Abrams, A. (2018, June 20). *Yes, Impostor Syndrome Is Real. Here's How to Deal With It.* Time; Time.
    https://time.com/5312483/
    how-to-deal-with-impostor-syndrome/

Begley, S. (2007, January 19). *The Brain: How The Brain Rewires Itself.* Time; Time.
    http://content.time.com/time/magazine/
    article/0,9171,1580438-1,00.html

Evers, K. (2012, June 1). *Finding the Zone.* Harvard Business Review.
    https://hbr.org/2012/06/finding-the-zone

Goudreau, J. (2016, January 16). *A Harvard psychologist says people judge you based on 2 criteria when they first meet you.* Business Insider.
    https://www.businessinsider.com/
    harvard-psychologist-amy-cuddy-how-people-judge-you-2016-1

Lowe, R., & Ziemke, T. (2011). The Feeling of Action Tendencies: On the Emotional Regulation of Goal-Directed Behavior. *Frontiers in Psychology, 2*(346). https://doi.org/10.3389/fpsyg.2011.00346

Muse, M. W.-T. (2017, May 18). The Five Types Of Impostor Syndrome And How To Beat Them. Fast Company https://www.fastcompany.com/40421352/the-five-types-of-impostor-syndrome-and-how-to-beat-them

O'Keefe, P. A., Dweck, C., & Walton, G. (2018, September 10). *Having a Growth Mindset Makes It Easier to Develop New Interests.* Harvard Business Review. https://hbr.org/2018/09/having-a-growth-mindset-makes-it-easier-to-develop-new-interests

Vilhauer Ph.D., J. (2019, December 31). *Why Spielberg, a Film School Reject, Was Successful Anyway.* Psychology Today. https://www.psychologytoday.com/us/blog/living-forward/201912/why-spielberg-film-school-reject-was-successful-anyway

Ward, M. (2017, January 29). 5 Things You Didn't Know About Oprah Winfrey. Vogue. https://www.vogue.com/article/oprah-winfrey-5-things-you-didnt-know

ABOUT THE AUTHOR

CHRISTINE SANNI...

Her story is unfinished. She continues to paint, create, imagine, dream, follow what inspires her, and work towards what calls her. She is not restricted by labels and believes that anything can be accomplished through hard work, commitment, and vision. As your Greatness Coach, Christine is committed to building a community that believes they have what it takes to leave the world a better place.

Committed to connecting and providing a platform for ALL to know and understand their GREATNESS.

MOTIVATIONAL QUOTES

It's never the mountain that stops you. It's simply that you stopped. Keep going.
Our greatest lessons are in the climb.

-Christine Sanni

I dare you to…
Ask more questions and seek more knowledge.

-Christine Sanni

I dare you to...
Trust yourself this time around.

-Christine Sanni

I dare you to…
Forgive and let go, not because it didn't hurt but
because it hurt and you're still here.
Know your strength.

-Christine Sanni

I dare you to...
Cry. Let it out. Allow yourself to feel again. Because
when you feel who you are
You have the power to feel who you can become.

-Christine Sanni

I dare you to...
Create what only you can see.

-Christine Sanni

I dare you to...
Love hard. Love deep down, beyond the surface.
Love humanity.

-Christine Sanni

I dare you to...
Believe that even if you fail, you will be better for it.

-Christine Sanni

I dare you to...
Share...Share who you truly are and inspire others
in a way
You would not have imagined.

-Christine Sanni

I dare you to...
Trust yourself this time around.

-Christine Sanni

I dare you to...
Try. Yes, I know it's hard and it feels like you are in this thing by yourself. But what matters right now, in this moment, is that you simply try.

-Christine Sanni

You are...
Creatively equipped.

-Christine Sanni

You are...
Trusted with greatness from birth.

-Christine Sanni

You are...
Capable of conquering the unknown.

-Chrisgtine Sanni

You are...
Positioned to grow beyond adversity, pain,
disappointment, judgment, and doubt.

-Christine Sanni

You are...
The author of your journey, a canvas worth painting.

-Christine Sanni

You are...
#greatlymade.

-Christine Sanni

No matter what your mountain looks like...
Run through it!

-Christine Sanni

Your Impact begins with just one step...You!
Collide with who you are.

-Christine Sanni

Whenever you have doubt or believe you have lost your way, remember who you are. What has life given you? Take that and use it to push you forward.

-Christine Sanni

May you create what has always been inside you.
Home, it's where creativity begins.

-Christine Sanni

Touch the world with the beauty of your authenticity
and the power of your flame.

-Christine Sanni

You have...
24 hours to create. To do the work. To positively impact others. To Give.

-Christine Sanni

There is purpose in it all.
Let your journey become your greatest motivator.

-Christine Sanni

Stay focused. Your purpose doesn't disappear because of a storm. In the noise and in the mess, your purpose, the reason you are here still matters. Yes, you must keep going.

-Christine Sanni

In any situation, it is you who has the power to choose
who you will be in that moment.
Stand in your power always.

-Christine Sanni

Happiness cannot be found, it must be created.
How do you create happiness? You give...
Without expectation...
And it is there, in that selfless act, that true happiness
is created within.

-Christine Sanni

Listen to what inspires you unexpectedly.

-Christine Sanni

Discovery starts with your belief.

-Christine Sanni

Outcomes start with your belief.

-Christine Sanni

MY LETTER TO FEAR

Dear Fear,

"I had to let you go."

Even though my heart and head often told me I could accomplish my dreams, I gave you the final say. Even in the smallest consideration you seemed to know me better than I knew myself. I trusted that you knew the outcome even though I had yet to test and develop my own grit. And even when I mustered up enough courage to pursue an idea, I chose to bring you along for the ride and doubt myself every step of the way. Despite getting to a certain point in life you still prevented me from seeing the tools I had already gained from my experiences.

You convinced me that I would fail and prevented me from seeing that failure equaled growth and would teach me my most powerful life lessons. You convinced me that I could only take the first step as long as I had a complete map of where I was going. You ruled my life. I stood by waiting for permission to explore the deepest parts of me; to run after all of my ambitions; and to understand the world from a different vantage point, outside my comfort zone.

But there came a day when I decided to do something different. I chose to believe in the unknown; to trust the process, no matter the outcome. I chose to believe that I would accomplish whatever I put my mind, heart, and soul into. And on that day, I realized what scared me the most was not that I would fail but that I would never see the change I was born to create.

Fear, you were wrong and always have been. So, I had to let you go.

I write this letter to say thank you.

Thank you for being there whenever my purpose seeks to show me the way. I now see that if my ambitions don't scare me they simply aren't big enough.

Fearless,

C.S.

P.S. Write your letter to fear.